CREATIVE CONSTRAINTS

CREATIVE
CONSTRAINTS

Translation and Authorship

Edited by Rita Wilson and Leah Gerber

Monash University Publishing
Building 4, Monash University
Clayton, Victoria 3800, Australia
www.publishing.monash.edu

Monash University Publishing brings to the world publications which advance the best traditions of humane and enlightened thought.

Monash University Publishing titles pass through a rigorous process of independent peer review.

Author: Wilson, Rita; Gerber, Leah (Eds)

Title: Creative Constraints: Translation and Authorship / Rita Wilson and Leah Gerber.

Edition: 1st ed.

ISBN: 9781921867897 (pb)
ISBN: 9781921867903 (web)

Subjects: Literary translation; Creative writing; Translation studies.

www.publishing.monash.edu/books/cc9781921867897.html

Design: Les Thomas

Cover image: copyright ©2012 iStockphoto LP. Image no. 2373867. *Burnt Antique Parchment* by AlexMax. Used with permission.

Printed in Australia by Griffin Press an Accredited ISO AS/NZS 14001:2004 Environmental Management System printer.

The paper this book is printed on is certified by the Programme for the Endorsement of Forest Certification scheme. Griffin Press holds PEFC chain of custody SGS - PEFC/COC-0594. PEFC promotes environmentally responsible, socially beneficial and economically viable management of the world's forests.

CONTENTS

PART II: CREATIVE PRACTICE

PART III: TRANSLATIONS

Acknowledgements

We would like to thank all those colleagues who during the peer review process provided valuable feedback on the contributions to this collection. We are also grateful to Elizabeth Bryer for her invaluable assistance in preparing the manuscript for publication. Grateful acknowledgement is made to the following for permission to reprint previously published material:

Alice Pung: excerpts from 'Multicultural women's day address' at alicepung.com/blog/. Copyright © 2008 by Alice Pung. Used by permission of Alice Pung.

Au vent des îsles: excerpts from *Le Roi absent* by Moetai Brotherson. Copyright © 2007 by Au vent des îsles. Used by permission of Au vent des îsles.

Black Inc.: excerpts from *Unpolished Gem* by Alice Pung. Copyright © 2006 by Alice Pung. Used by permission of Black Inc.

Beltz & Gelberg: excerpts from *Wie ein Vogel im Käfig* by Heike Brandt. Copyright © 1992, 2003 by Beltz & Gelberg. Used by permission of Beltz & Gelberg.

Ediciones Libertarias: excerpts from *La caza del Snark* by Lewis Carroll, translated by Leopoldo María Panero. Translation copyright © 1982 by Ediciones Libertarias. Used by permission of Ediciones Libertarias.

Éditions P.O.L.: excerpts from *Kub Or* by Pierre Alferi. Copyright © 1994 by Éditions P.O.L. Used by permission of Éditions P.O.L.

Jacket Magazine: 'Ardour'. Copyright © by 2008 John Kinsella. Used by permission of John Kinsella.

Little Island: for permission to publish a translation of an extract of *Le Roi absent*, for which they hold English translation rights.

Penguin Group: excerpt from *The Tale of Genji* by Murasaki Shikibu, translated by Royall Tyler. Translation copyright © 2001 by Royall Tyler. Used by permission of Penguin Group (UK) and by permission of Viking Penguin, a division of Penguin Group (USA).

Princeton University Press: excerpt from *What Is World Literature?* by David Damrosch. Copyright © 2003 by Princeton University Press. Used by permission of Princeton University Press.

Random House Mondadori: excerpt from *Los muertos* by Jorge Carrión. Copyright © 2010 by Random House Mondadori. Used by permission of Random House Mondadori.

Introduction

Rita Wilson and Leah Gerber

The emergence of translation studies as an academic discipline – with a concomitant focus on the variable status of the literary translator – has led to an intensified interest in the creative process of translation and an emphasis on the translator's creativity and autonomy as a producer of literary culture. Theorising creativity, as Manuela Perteghella and Eugenia Loffredo remind us in their volume on literary translation and creative writing, 'has always been a daunting task' (2006, 8). Nevertheless in the last decade there have been a number of attempts to understand creativity in the specific context of translation.[1] Recent studies that have brought to the fore parallels between the dynamics of translation and those of creative writing have paid particular attention to the relationship between the creative freedom enjoyed by the translator and the multiplicity of constraints to which translation as process and product is necessarily subject. Clive Scott, a renowned scholar in the fields of comparative literature and translation studies, argues in favour of an approach to translation that sees it as activity rather than as product, and as a bringing into being of the potentialities of a source text, in and through (a version) of the target text. Scott contends that 'all texts that survive owe that survival to their capacity to ramify and diversify, intralingually, interlingually and intersemiotically' (2009, 39). The traffic, in terms of increased interest in the overlapping conceptions and practices of translation and creative writing, is not merely uni-directional.

This collection of essays aims to illustrate the parallel and overlapping discourses within the cognate areas of literary studies, creative writing and translation studies, which have come together to propose a view of translation as (a form of) creative writing and creative writing as being shaped by translation processes. Such a view has been enabled, *inter alia*, by a re-inscription of relations between writer and reader and an enhanced understanding of the dynamics of reading and writing. Referring to his

---

1   In addition to the chapters by Kussmaul and Ñarčević in Chesterman, Gallardo San Salvador and Gambier (2000), several edited volumes have been dedicated to this topic: cf. Bassnett and Bush (2005), Kemble and O'Sullivan (2006), Perteghella, and Loffredo, (2006). See also Pommer (2008).

own experience as a novelist and literary translator, Tim Parks explains the value of translation to his authorial work by drawing attention to how translation forces close reading of the text, background research and a search for coherence: 'the hands-on experience [for the translator] of how another writer puts together his work is worth a year's creative writing classes' (Parks 2010). The essays in this volume explore the relationship between translators and authors in its various manifestations, from the author–translator collaboration, to self-translation, and to authorial practices of translating. Recent research in the history of self-translation has shown that it continues to be a widespread phenomenon in several cultures and is closely linked to the representation of the self. The contributors draw on a wide variety of genres, cultures and languages, maintaining a balance between the theory and the practice of literary translation. In doing so, they explore the links among creative writing, (self-)translation and creative practice in translation. The latter activity, in particular, interrogates the constraints placed on the translator by promoting collaboration in a variety of forms, including placing translators and authors in open dialogue.

Several of the contributions in this volume are written by participants of *Translated!*, the inaugural Literary Translation Summer School, run under the auspices of the School of Languages, Cultures and Linguistics at Monash University in collaboration with the British Centre for Literary Translation (BCLT) in February 2011. The workshops provided a unique opportunity for translators to explore their interpretations of the source text by posing questions to the authors present, which revealed the inherent ambiguities of any literary analysis. This process also reinforced the value of a creative approach to literary translation and highlighted the complex relationship between the notion of authorship and an original text.

The opening essay of the collection by Valerie Henitiuk, current director of the BCLT, is based on the address she delivered at the launch of this event. Henitiuk begins by considering the properties of refraction, reminding us that the term is normally used to describe light or sound waves, which become oblique as they encounter the boundary between media of different densities. She points out that spectacular natural phenomena, such as rainbows, or the splitting of white light into many colours as it passes through a glass prism and disperses, are also the result of refraction. She goes on to argue that refraction is a surprisingly useful concept for examining how texts, upon being translated, angle off in a different direction from the path of origin, how they adapt to new forms and take on new significances, and how this enables monolingual English speakers to read something quite different in form and style from what the West understands as belonging to the novelistic genre.

Henitiuk teases out what it might mean to understand literary translation, retranslation and their related creative by-products as being indebted to an inherently refractive process. In so doing, she provides a springboard for Ramón López Castellano's ruminations on the *poète maudit* of contemporary Spanish letters, Leopoldo María Panero. Panero, who has devoted his life to literature, constructing an immense, radical and unique corpus of poetry unparalleled in Spanish literature, has not limited himself to poetic production per se; he has produced some of the most daring pages in Spanish on literary criticism and literary translation. Panero terms the notion and practice of translation 'per-version': that is, the inherently organic nature of translation as literary (re)creation and proliferation, equal, if not better, to the process of 'original' creation. 'Per-version' is regarded as a necessary and independent progression that engulfs both texts and authors and that ultimately reveals the essential mechanisms of literature.

The relationship between literary (re)creation and translation is explored from another perspective in Rita Wilson's analysis of processes of self-translation in the literary production of four contemporary Italophone women writers. She examines these writers' discursive and linguistic explorations of bi- or multilingualism, and the literary forms they employ to negotiate the migration experience. Wilson pays particular attention to the writers' own reflections on how the shift in languages has affected their way of perceiving and understanding themselves, and their new reality. She offers tangible examples of how individuals engage with multilingual and increasingly globalised culture by performing creative transformations of self. Wilson argues that examining the self-translating process within literary texts offers insights into cultural differences and commonalities, as well as revealing the potential that these writers' linguistic diversity has for opening up new sources of literary creativity by renewing literary language and traditions.

Ouyang Yu expands on many of these issues in his essay 'Giving birth to the self: On self-translation'. Ouyang is an established writer, poet and literary translator who provides a particularly insightful discussion on self-translation, a literary translational genre with which he has been engaged for more than twenty years. Yet Ouyang finds that self-translation has left him feeling 'ashamed' and 'degraded' because of the scant attention – both critical and creative – given to the genre, and due to the minimal space given to its publication in either language. Ouyang argues that literary self-translation, which involves, in his case, fiction and poetry translated from Chinese into English (and vice versa), is vital to the existence and survival of the writer-translator, and that it presents a kind of re-creation akin to rebirth in another tongue. This process is demonstrated with reference to a number of Ouyang's self-translated poems from the Chinese language as well as an example of a collaborative self-translation between him and poet John Kinsella, with the Chinese-language scripts incorporated in the text.

Although Lia Hills considers many similar issue facing the writer when practising self-translation, the main focus of her contribution is the rapport that develops between an author's own writing and that of the other when engaging in a work of translation, and how, in the process, the 'self' is translated into the new work. The suggestion is that though the writer's sense of self as practitioner, and of her own writing, is both challenged and enriched through contact with the language of the other, it is essential that the writer endeavour to maintain her own voice in order for the translation to be authentic. Ways in which the writer can avoid 'losing herself' in the language of the other are considered, with the aim being to emerge from the experience of translation with a greater sense of embodiment, of presence in the writer's own language. Hills also highlights the similarities between the processes of the writer and the translator. Though the core of the paper is drawn from the author's own experience, the practices of writer-translators such as Ezra Pound are also discussed, as is the role that translation played in shaping their language and style.

In the second part of the volume, the focus moves to the creative practice of the literary translator. Adele D'Arcangelo's chapter reflects on her translation into Italian of Australian author Alice Pung's bestselling memoir *Unpolished Gem* (2006), providing a unique insight into translation as communication rather than as an act of transfer. D'Arcangelo observes that the translator is thus acknowledged as operating in a decision-making space related to both the construction of meaning in the source text and the creation of meaning in the target text. The process of cultural transposition is discussed with reference to Lawrence Venuti's concept of the (in)visibility of the translator and to metaphors used by writers and critics such as Homi Bhabha, Salman Rushdie and Pilar Godayol to describe the translation–negotiation process. D'Arcangelo argues that translating Pung's 'across the borders' experience into Italian asks the translator to locate a 'space of hybridity' within the target language and culture, hence redefining cross-linguistic perspectives on one side, but mostly encouraging multicultural encounters for potential target readers on the other.

While D'Arcangelo tackles Pung's often ironic expression, as well as the effect of estrangement created by Pung's skilful fusing of Australian English and Chinese, Jean Anderson looks for creative solutions to the untranslatability of humour. Theorists have paid relatively little attention to the translation of humour, and even less to the issues encountered in the translation of postcolonial humour. She considers how Tahitian writer Moetai Brotherson deploys a range of strategies to comic effect in *Le Roi absent* (2007), including the juxtaposing references from a number of cultures, both European and indigenous. Shakespeare's 'My kingdom for a horse' is closely followed by The Muppet Show's 'Pigs in space'; a chess tournament references 'Gunfight at the OK Corral'; an erotic encounter evokes biblical stories; and Polynesian students in Paris assert their attachment to the Place Saint Michel through a traditional cultural practice. By examining the use of humour-generating juxtapositions, Anderson shows the comic elements may well be closely related to the issues of cultures in contact and the imbalance of power between them, and argues that this is a framework the translator must keep firmly in focus.

Finally, drawing together the various aspects of the art and craft of literary translation, award-winning literary translator and former director of the BCLT, Peter Bush, provides illuminating insights on an activity that he considers central to the very existence of human culture. Bush highlights the importance of collaboration in this complex process, giving emphasis to the interplay between editor and translator. The focus of his contribution is on the complexities and sensitivities involved in translating for publication, and how those interactions, as recorded in drafts, edits and parallel translations, may relate to the education of literary translators. His essay also provides the context for the final section of the volume, which features translations produced during the week-long translation workshops at the *Translated!* Summer School.

Each workshop was led by an acclaimed translator and the author of the text, giving rise to lively discussions and debates around strategies to address translation challenges, as well as emphasising the value of author–translator collaboration. Led by Jean Anderson, the group of French translators took on excerpts from the celebrated novel, *Le Roi absent* ('The Missing King' 2007) by Tahitian author Moetai Brotherson. The text is split into two parts, each with a different narrator-protagonist, creating a weaving together of multiple eras and voices, and differing perspectives on narratives about and from the Pacific. The Spanish translators tackled parts of Jorge Carrión's experimental crime novel, *Los muertos* ('The Dead' 2010), assisted by Peter

Bush. A book about death and memory, *Los muertos* is Carrión's debut novel, and the first volume of a thematically rich trilogy. The German group adopted a different approach: it translated *Wie ein Vogel im Käfig* ('Like a Bird in a Cage' 1991) by writer, translator and critic Heike Brandt into English, with the assistance of renowned Australian children's author, Elizabeth Honey. Brandt's text explores the relationship between a German girl, Rebecca, and a Turkish boy, Halef, in Kreuzberg, the 'melting-pot' suburb of Berlin, not long after the fall of the Wall. The perhaps untapped potential for author–translator collaboration is acutely emphasised by Brandt and Honey, who enjoy a unique working relationship, having co-written the popular children's novel, *To the Boy in Berlin* (2007). The German group came face-to-face with many challenges in translating for children, and were also able to put into practice some of their new-found strategies by translating some of Honey's recent work from English into German.

The translations of these recent French, Spanish and German literary works mirror the conversations conducted by our various contributors on the creative constraints involved in literary translation. The volume draws attention to translation's place in contemporary literature, a topic that is central to the current debates around notions of 'world literature'. Delineating approaches that contest the traditional notion of translation as a secondary activity, the contributors to the volume propose that, in many cases, a process of 'intertextual grafting' takes place, so that the translator's work mirrors and complements that of the creative writer. The notions of translations as 'refractions', 'transcreations' and 'per-versions' discussed within the theoretical contributions to the volume affirm the nature of translations both as literary (re)creations and creative transformations of self.

References

Bassnett, Susan; Bush, Peter, eds. 2005. *The Translator as Writer*. London/New York: Continuum.

Bush, Peter. 2011. 'From *Los muertos* by Jorge Carrión'. Trans. Translation Workshop Students under the direction of Bush, Peter. *The Quarterly Conversation* (24). Accessed 20 November 2011. Available from: http://quarterlyconversation.com/from-los-muertos-by-jorge-carrion.

Kemble, Ian; O'Sullivan, Carol, eds. 2006. *Translation and Creativity: How Creative is the Translator?* Portsmouth: University of Portsmouth. 72–81.

Parks, Tim. 2010. 'Why translators deserve some credit'. *The Observer* 25 April. Accessed 4 May 2012. Available from: http://www.guardian.co.uk/books/2010/apr/25/book-translators-deserve-credit.

Perteghella, Manuela; Loffredo, Eugenia, eds. 2006. *Translation and Creativity: Perspectives on Creative Writing and Translation Studies*. London/New York: Continuum.

Pommer, Sieglinde E. 2008. 'No creativity in legal translation?' *Babel. Revue internationale de la traduction* 54 (4): 355–368.

Kussmaul, Paul. 2000. 'Types of creative translating.' In *Translation in Context*, edited by Chesterman, Andrew; Gallardo San Salvador, Natividad; Gambier, Yves. Amsterdam/Philadelphia: John Benjamins: 117–126.

Ńarčević, Susan. 2000. 'Creativity in legal translation: How much is too much?' In *Translation in Context*, edited by Chesterman, Andrew; Gallardo San Salvador, Natividad; Gambier, Yves. Amsterdam/Philadelphia: John Benjamins: 281–292.

Scott, Clive. 2009. 'From linearity to tabularity'. *CTIS Occasional Papers* Vol. 4. Manchester: The University of Manchester: 37–53.

Part I

Transcreation and self-translation

Chapter 1

Optical illusions?

Literary translation as a refractive process

Valerie Henitiuk

Refraction involves the turning or bending of something as it passes from one medium into another, the term normally being used of light or sound waves, which become oblique as they encounter the boundary between media of different densities. The wave's velocity is affected by this change in medium; the wavelength changes (increasing or decreasing depending on circumstances), although the frequency may remain the same. Refraction tends to create optical illusions, for which our brains have learned to compensate – we 'know' that a pencil standing in a glass of water is not really broken or that objects below the surface of a lake are not quite as large as they may appear. More spectacular natural phenomena such as rainbows, or the splitting of white light into many colours as it passes through a glass prism and disperses (its various components each taking a different angle), are also the result of refraction. The colour spectrum constitutes the visible manifestation of the existing range of wavelengths. It was Newton who taught us that all those colours are not created by the prism, as was previously believed, but rather that they are naturally contained within the light itself.

I cannot help but find this concept to be a surprisingly useful one for working through the following: how texts angle off in a different direction from the path of origin upon being translated; how texts adapt to new forms and take on new significances; and how we are able to read, in English, something quite different in form and style from what the West understands as belonging to the novelistic genre and yet speak, in all seriousness, of reading a Japanese novel. This chapter, therefore, will tease out what it might mean to understand the debt of literary translation, retranslation and their related creative by-products to an inherently refractive process. If we look at translational activity in terms of a prism that functions to reveal a range of colours or interpretations, can this help us avoid some of the more common traps of the perennially over-simplifying dichotomy of domestication versus foreignisation or literal versus free? Can we usefully view a given source text's offshoots in other languages and cultures as various manifestations of the spectrum already potentially present in an original work of literature?

My research interests lie within the framework of world literature, a discipline originally named by Goethe, promoted by Karl Marx, and which is now rapidly gaining ground across the world. Recent scholarship by David Damrosch and Pascale Casanova addresses vital contemporary issues such as globalisation, canon formation, and the eternal struggle for cultural dominance in terms of what and how we read. Damrosch highlights the specific term with which I opened this chapter in his threefold definition from 2003 (281), characterising world literature as: (1) an elliptical refraction of national literatures; (2) literature that gains in translation; and (3) a mode of reading rather than a set canon. Of course, because human beings are fallible interpreters, some of the manifestations based on what we are able to understand of works from a context outside our own will inevitably be less reliable than others – perhaps resulting in an egregious misreading or, to carry on with the optical metaphor, a sort of mirage. Nevertheless, by studying how and why particular representations arise, irrespective of questions of mere fidelity, we may well learn something valuable about the original as well as about the transformative process it undergoes as it circulates far from home. This chapter argues that the refractive impulse and the translative gain that Damrosch rightly describes as important facets of any literature read cross-culturally are in fact far more intertwined than he suggests. As a text is being read in a language, medium, or juxtaposition other than that of its origin, together they expose and give scope to previously unseen significances and allow new intertextualities to develop. And that particular mode of reading, Damrosch proposes, is in fact an essential part of how every translation is produced and thus how an ancient Japanese text at long last takes its rightful place within the 'world republic of letters' (Casanova 2004).

Ubaldo Stecconi has recently asked, 'What happens if we think that translating is a wave?' (2009, 47) Rejecting the old model whereby the meaning or message is a static thing that is simply picked up and carried over, Stecconi argues for translation as, instead, a 'non-linear cognitive process' (2009, 57) involving a dynamic passage of energy. As he explains:

'when a wave leaves – say – the coast of Dalmatia and reaches Ancona across the Adriatic Sea, not a single drop of water moves west. Water particles that find themselves in the path of the wave move up and down as the wave goes through' (54–55).

The characteristic properties of waves, whether of water or of light, thus provide a way of understanding the translative process as not one of mere transfer, but instead of an exchange of energy that, within certain constraints, brings us entirely new texts. Interestingly, according to Stecconi's model, 'refraction could correspond to the feeling of material resistance translators experience at the interface between different semiotic systems' (Stecconi 2009, 56), a resistance that can give rise to inspired creativity.

Some two decades ago, André Lefevere published an essay titled 'Mother Courage's Cucumbers: Text, System and Refraction in a Theory of Literature', which was later reprinted in Lawrence Venuti's widely read *Translation Studies Reader*. An insightful study of how Brechtian poetics have come to be accepted within the English theatrical canon and more broadly of how translations operate within the global literary polysystem, Lefevere's essay relates to my thinking about where 'translation' and 'refraction' may fruitfully coincide. Lefevere's focus and mine differ, however, in that his primary objective is to refute the Romantic theory of literary originality. Further, he limits his discussion of refractions to instances of 'translation, criticism, and historiography' (Lefevere 2004, 244) and fails to engage seriously with the meaning of this provocative term. While I am indebted to this earlier essay on certain levels, particularly regarding the vital role translations play in the overall evolution of literatures, my goal here is to engage more fully with this notion of translative refraction and explore the degree to which it can serve to advance current theorising about how world literature is and should be read. I am also determined to set aside as distinctly unhelpful any characterisation of a given translator's specific choices as simply or even primarily 'misunderstandings and misconceptions' (Lefevere 2004, 240).

As suggested above, my own corpus for analysis tends to be drawn from Japanese literature, particularly as researched and taught in the West by leading scholars such as Haruo Shirane, who has written extensively of the modern 'invention' of Japan's canon, as well as of the range of media in which these pre-modern texts now exist and are read. I work a great deal with women's writing of the Heian period, which covers roughly the eighth to the twelfth centuries, and its intercultural reception. Naturally, translation studies must deeply inform any study of the ongoing re-creation of these classical works of literature as they travel to and within the modern West. Seminal books by Edwin Gentzler, Theo Hermans, Maria Tymoczko and others have begun challenging us to envision translation in a far more nuanced fashion and have forced a profound rethinking of our presuppositions about the models and processes involved, as well as the impacts thereof. The role of the translator can no longer be seen as anything like self-evident or tangential, and the interdisciplinary approach demanded by any world literature theorising worthy of the name engages usefully with how and why that should be so.

The greatest and most beloved artefact of all Japanese letters is *The Tale of Genji*, a long and psychologically complex work authored a millennium ago by a woman known today as Murasaki Shikibu. Although not fully appreciated by the first Europeans introduced to it in the mid-nineteenth century, by the early twentieth century this story of a prince and the varied and fascinating women around whom his life is centred had already become widely acknowledged as a global masterpiece. Now, as we mark the millennial anniversary of its original creation, we can look back on not only the native development of this foundational work of Japanese literature, but also a distinct, independent Western reception history that comprises some 130 years of its telling and retelling. The *Genji* has taken on a new and often surprising life through its positioning by translators within the medium of English (my discussion will be confined to this target language, although that text's existence in many languages of the West is closely connected).

In Japanese, Murasaki Shikibu's great classic is known as *Genji Monogatari*, with *monogatari* meaning 'tale' or 'tales'. Number is not specified in that language and, despite the fossilised title by which we have long come to know the work (in both English and other Western languages), it actually makes more sense to read this as a plural noun. What the author offers us are numerous, over-layered tales, all connected through a Genji – again, contrary to popular misconceptions, this is an honorary title rather than a proper name. A *genji* is a member of the imperial family who has been excluded for whatever reason from the line of succession, which is true of the primary male character. This character, whom we nonetheless tend to refer to as Genji or the Shining Genji, dies about two-thirds of the way through the work, and the adventures from that point on are related to Kaoru, his purported son. Not a few scholars in recent years, especially those working from a consciously feminist or post-modern stance, accordingly argue that neither Genji nor Kaoru should be seen as the hero of the tale or tales, but instead that they function as merely access points to the great variety of remarkable women they encounter. As I argue in a previously published article (Henitiuk 2008) and will touch on below, the fact that virtually all of the text's translators have been male should not go unnoticed, as this has had a significant impact on how many of its elements have come to be read and understood.

While Murasaki Shikibu is recognised both inside and outside Japan as an important literary figure, the Western response to not only her writing but also her authorial presence has not infrequently been perplexed and perplexing. Late-nineteenth-century Europeans faced very real challenges of inadequate preparation for the generic, stylistic and linguistic difference of Japanese letters, but were nonetheless intrigued to learn more about the country's classical writing and not a little titillated by the notion of a woman writing openly of amorous adventures. These early scholar-diplomats were rightly taken aback by the centuries' worth of hitherto undiscovered artistic wealth produced by Japan, until so recently closed to the West, and passages from the incommensurable *Genji* were among the very first chosen for translation into Western languages. The paths by which this text has since been received by an English-speaking audience have been multiple, even convoluted, and today we are spoiled for choice with versions ranging from close prose renderings to homages in verse, and adaptations for stage or screen, visual arts and music.

Adaptations and imitations tamper extensively with both form and substance, self-consciously offering anything but a neutral reading, but translations are also subjective by nature. Certainly with literary works, translation is implicitly if not explicitly re-creative (in both senses of the term), a process whereby the constraints under which the translator must operate are different in kind from those typically impinging on the translator of a technical manual, for example, or perhaps of a religious tract. French translator Serge Gavronsky's distinction between pietistic and cannibalistic translation may be a helpful framework when thinking about the parameters of any rewriting practice. In the former, the original is held as sacred, and thus the translator's role is necessarily secondary and strictly controlled, while in the latter, an autonomous translator cannibalises or exploits that original, transforming (or refracting) it in myriad creative ways. Unfortunately, far too much translator training and discussion about translations continues to take the 'sacredness' of any literary text as a given, despite overwhelming evidence that no translation is ever objective or transparent. The *Genji* in English has been extensively cannibalised, and we need to recognise this process as natural to literary globalisation.

Homi Bhabha once described translation as 'how newness enters the world', and certainly renditions by Suematsu Kenchô (at the time transcribed as Suyematz Kenchio) in 1882 and Arthur Waley in the 1920s and 1930s were consciously introducing something quite novel to a Western readership, feeling obliged to rework and recontextualise as they rewrote for a non-Japanese audience. Suematsu, among the first native Japanese to study at Cambridge, published an abridged version of the *Genji* that marked its initial appearance in English, with the explicit aim of establishing his nation as a major cultural player equal to Victorian England and other colonial powers. Waley took up the task some 30 years later and developed his own, independent vision of Murasaki Shikibu's masterpiece as an aesthetic artefact, firmly placed within the current of European modernism.

In 1976, American Edward Seidensticker sought to rectify some of Waley's quite striking idiosyncrasies (the British translator had elaborated on many passages seemingly at will, for example, but also excised important scenes that he deemed would lack any interest for his readers) with an updated version, which was to remain the standard for students and general readers for a quarter of a century. His reading remains extremely popular despite often clunky stylistic choices that are sharply at odds with the author's languid, labyrinthine prose. Another translation of ten chapters of the *Genji* (along with a dozen or so from the *Tale of the Heike*) appeared in 1994, targeted by the Classical Japanese scholar, Helen Craig McCullough, specifically for university classroom use. Although intelligently and sensitively done, this abridgement is not generally read outside the academic context. In 2001, Royall Tyler took advantage of present-day readers' greater level of comfort with much that had once seemed unutterably foreign in terms of style, literary conventions and cultural references, and released what is arguably the most accurate English rendering to date; but it has yet to unseat fully the long-established versions done by Waley and Seidensticker.

Each of these five translations reads quite differently, but – as Lefevere also argues on behalf of Brecht's successive interpreters – the difference inherent to the versions 'lies not with the dictionary... it is not one of semantic equivalence' (2004, 248). While competently interpreting Murasaki Shikibu's great tale and revealing particular aspects of its beauty, they also reveal their own preoccupations, conditioned by the very different worlds in which they lived and worked – altering the wavelength even as they maintain the basic frequency, in other words.

It should be underscored that most of these re-creations have themselves served as source texts for translation into various other languages, thereby contributing directly to a complex and constantly evolving phenomenon world-wide. Even more significantly, although I do not have space here to deal with the feedback loop in any detail, it was in many ways owing to Western retellings of and passion for Japan's canonical literature that this native masterpiece also enjoyed a revival at home, culminating in what is commonly referred to as today's 'Genji bu-mu'. Many Japanese authors have written of coming to appreciate their notoriously difficult pre-modern literary inheritance through Waley's early twentieth-century English translation. Since at least that time, Murasaki Shibibu's modern descendants have learned to celebrate the *Genji* as very much a living text, one that has been made immensely readable in recent decades through modernisations by Tanizaki Junichiro or Setouchi Jakuchô, for example. It has also thereby become fully available for adaptation into popular novels, poetry, theatre, film, manga and even video games.

Murasaki Shikibu's unforgettable characters and themes have subsequently been taken up by creative writers, artists and composers in many Western cultures as well, further refracting the eleventh-century original. In English, we have *Genji* plays, operas, jazz compositions, dance performances, art books, countless poems and blogs. Her text has also inspired novelists as disparate as Iris Murdoch (who playfully develops something akin to a polyandrous harem in the English countryside in *The Nice and the Good*) or Edmund White (who uses elements of the Japanese tale to craft the story of a gay community à la Fire Island, imbued with a surreal, dreamlike atmosphere, in his *Forgetting Elena*). A more recent novel, *Tale of Murasaki* by Liza Dalby, seeks to reverse-engineer the story of the Heian Japanese author's life through episodes recounted in her text.

The series of six stunning woodblock prints made by American artist Helen Frankenthaler offers yet another refracted angle of dissemination. I find it interesting that the series is titled *Tales of Genji*, and like to believe that by this plural she intended to mark their participation in a distinctly multifaceted, and potentially unending, creative endeavour. Be that as it may, the following lines from the exhibition catalogue for her prints serve to summarise what the best of these more distant refractions may achieve: 'Vivid color, rich texture, painstaking attention to detail are qualities that the non-representational art of Helen Frankenthaler and the incident-laden *Tale of Genji* have in common. The woodcuts won't tell us a thing about the book's plot, but they tell us a lot about the sensation of reading it' (Edenbaum 2004, 2).

It is a fact that our senses cannot always be trusted to pass along information in any reliable way; such is even more the case when the object being perceived, received and rewritten arose from a culture and worldview vastly removed from our own, not to mention already once refracted by a translator. Let us pause here for a moment to consider further some of the ways that refraction can and does distort, presenting images that, while entertaining or tantalising, do not necessarily have much to do with what is really in front of us.

Related to that bent pencil in the glass of water are other optical phenomena such as mirages and Fata Morgana. As with reflections in a mirror (to which the term is etymologically related), but more so, a mirage shows images of things that are not where or as they appear to be. The enticing pool of water appearing to hover just ahead of us in the desert or above the road is a product of heat differential between the ground and the surrounding air: as light passes from cooler to suddenly warmer air, it refracts and produces a displaced and distorted image. Fata Morgana, named after King Arthur's shape-shifting half-sister, oddly allow us to see objects such as an island or ship that are below the horizon and thus that should not actually be available to our vision. These objects, which are often described as looking like fairytale castles, appear elevated, elongated and, even more oddly, inverted. Both phenomena are in fact quite real – unlike hallucinations, mirages and Fata Morgana can be photographed or filmed, for instance – but of course what observers understand of them is very much dependant on what they are hoping or prepared to see.

Through similarly inspired and inspiring refractions, various images of the *Genji* have become established as a fundamental, if more or less displaced, part of our global cultural heritage. A vast range of translations, retranslations, adaptations and imitations suggest how 'worlded' this Japanese classic has become, so readily available as the basis for other works of art – including what are often weird and wonderful interpretations by Western authors, poets, filmmakers and artists, as well as bloggers, academics and pornographers. These distortions have the capacity to allow us greater insight, to see more than we should be able to see (as with a Fata Morgana); they should never be dismissed as a mere mirage and thus something to be discounted. Of course, the very diversity of readings, which range from the cautiously accurate to the seriously misinformed, urges us to think carefully about just how fully assimilated any text can become by an audience located so far distant in time, space and worldview from that first addressed by the author.

So where do we locate this or any translated text? Where and how do we position ourselves as readers, and against what criteria do we try to comprehend it? Should we marvel at the exotic and hold it apart as inherently Other, or naïvely assume an underlying similarity? Damrosch helpfully presents a third possibility for consideration: reading within what he terms an 'elliptical' space, namely one that allows us to enjoy access to a work simultaneously from two distinct vantage points. As he puts it, the reading of world literature has traditionally:

> oscillated between extremes of assimilation and discontinuity: either the earlier and distant works reflect a consciousness *just like ours*, or they are unutterably alien, curiosities whose foreignness finally tells us nothing and can only reinforce our sense of separate identity. But why should we have to choose...? We never truly cease to be ourselves as we read, and our present concerns and modes of reading will always provide one focus of our understanding, but the literature of other times and eras presents us with another focus as well, and we read in the field of force generated between these two foci. (Damrosch 2003, 133)

However, this powerful 'field of force' can of course be successfully generated only when and if we read with awareness of where a world is both like and unlike our own, not only conscious of the dangerous lure of false identification, but also ready and willing to read against our ingrained cultural conditioning. Such an interpretative approach has great potential for increasingly sophisticated reading practice, but as with the sometimes unsettling visual effects of refraction, it remains a challenge for our brains to reconcile what our senses perceive with what is really there.

Successful negotiating with similarity and difference is key to comprehending any new literary text:

> Even a single work of literature is the locus of a negotiation between two different cultures. The receiving culture can use the foreign material in all sorts of ways... World literature is thus always as much about the host culture's values and needs as it is about a work's source culture; hence it is a double refraction, one that can be described through the figure of the ellipse..., connected to both cultures, circumscribed by neither alone. (Damrosch 2003, 283)

Although he is not speaking here of translation per se, I consider Damrosch's description of doubled cultural foci very useful for explaining the disorientation as well as the incredible cultural potential unleashed by the act of translating. A unilingual re-edition may highlight how an older English novel coincides with contemporary concerns, especially if it is accompanied by a critical introduction or commentary. With a text originally composed in a foreign language, however, a great deal of this 'domesticating' work will be effectively done through the translation process, as the rewriter's choices consciously or subconsciously bear witness to his or her own social and cultural context. I am not here advocating domestication but merely pointing out the difficulty any translator has in resisting a lifetime of socio-cultural training – even a determinedly foreignising approach will be constructed in many ways so as to fit the target culture. The reception of any translated text must be different in kind from that of its original: the foreign work has been brought into our space and we necessarily understand it against our own national traditions and the concerns of the day.

One way to illustrate how what I have been describing as a doubling of past and present, here and there, us and them may be manifested is through the close, critical reading of retranslations, or serial translations – each one of which will reveal a unique locus in the time and culture of the target text's production even as each successive wave faithfully 'carries across' the source text. To say that a translator cannot and does not function in a vacuum is of course not in any way meant as a criticism – refracted waves by definition suffer a change in direction and move obliquely. To be oblique means literally to be slanted or inclined, in other words neither parallel nor perpendicular – obliqueness thus often implies subterfuge, as when someone gives evasive answers to questions or when Emily Dickinson urges poets to 'tell all the truth / but tell it slant'. In the case of translation, or any reading at the interface between cultures, however, it is a necessary and positive condition of the act.

Through the refractive work first set in motion by Suematsu, and carried on by successive generations of translators, Japanese has undergone that important process by which a previously invisible literary tradition is transformed into an effective player on the global stage. As Pascale Casanova explains the process she calls 'littérisation':

> Literary transmutation is achieved by crossing a magic frontier that allows a text composed in an unprestigious language – or even a nonliterary language, which is to say one that either does not exist or is unrecognized in the verbal marketplace – to pass into a literary language. (2004, 136)

This so-called 'incarnation [as] literature' (137) in the eyes of the greater world of an inherently foreign masterpiece such as the *Genji* can occur only via translation, about which quite mystifyingly Casanova has virtually nothing to say in her lengthy and important book. It is nevertheless no small matter that the Murasaki Shikibu we know in English is de facto the invention of her translators, through whose elliptical readings so many Western readers at so many different times have gained an appreciation for her genius. The 'making literary' of a foreign work generally neither happens in one fell swoop, nor yet is it purely a linguistic matter; several refractions needed to occur before enough of the *Genji*'s spectrum was made visible to effect the international canonisation this Japanese text enjoys today. I am not interested in arguing here for a teleological progression, where more recent readings are assumed to be 'better'. Rather, I propose that each has something to teach us about the doubled perspective world literature demands and makes possible.

Looking now briefly to the opening lines of the *Genji Monogatari*, we are immediately confronted with some of the ways that each translator has coped with his own elliptical stance in constructing a particular refraction for English-language readers. To begin, let us see how the passage, in which we are introduced to the imperial court and the low-ranking woman generally known as Fujitsubo who will later give birth to Genji, was first rendered into English by Japanese native Suematsu almost 130 years ago:

> In the reign of a certain Emperor, whose name is unknown to us, there was, among the Niogo and Kôyi of the Imperial Court, one who, though she was not of high birth, enjoyed the full tide of Royal favor. Hence her superiors, each one of whom had always been thinking – 'I shall be the *one*,' gazed upon her disdainfully with malignant eyes, and her equals and inferiors were more indignant still.
>
> Such being the state of affairs, the anxiety which she had to endure was great and constant, and this was probably the reason why her health was at last so much affected, that she was often compelled to absent herself from Court, and to retire to the residence of her mother. (Suyematsu 1882, 1)

Suematsu overtly assumes the role of propagandist with this translation, prefaced by a polemical introduction arguing firmly for his country's advanced civilisation. He is eager (to borrow Damrosch's terminology) for the 'receiving culture' of Britain to accept this 'foreign material' as a sign of Japan's advanced state of civilisation some 800 years previously. Suematsu here gives us the *Genji* as a historical document, one that will prove Japan's longstanding cultural sophistication, and present its people as scientifically literate (for example, the botanist reference, which is clearly designed to appeal to Victorian fashions). Note also how he dissuades us from reading these lines as wholly fictional, opting instead to imply that the Emperor was a real personage whose name has simply not survived for posterity. Further, Suematsu does not hesitate to employ Japanese terms for which there are no obvious English equivalents, simply providing a brief footnote about the unfamiliar court titles. And that 'us' so near the beginning functions strategically in this context, the referent cannily shifting from Murasaki Shikibu's original audience to Suematsu's Victorian readers, underscoring the unknowability of the text, inherent to the pleasure of reading.

Despite being dismissed by Western Japanologists as merely a 'creditable performance under the circumstances' (Aston 1897–98, 285), Suematsu's version plays an absolutely vital role in making more than just a handful of excerpts from the *Genji* available; his work in fact appeared in several different editions and was even translated into German in 1911. Nonetheless, these pioneering efforts could go only so far at the time, when 'things Japanese' (see Chamberlain 1890) were so new to the West. His successor was the great Japanologist and Sinologist Arthur Waley, whose translation of the *Genji* has by contrast been hugely influential, used as a source text for many retranslations, and remains widely read even today. In the interwar years, readers were warmly disposed to welcome a highly aestheticised, that is, non-bellicose view of Japan and her culture, and Waley, as a member of the Bloomsbury group, both responded to and fostered that demand. His version strengthened that focus of the ellipsis that established the *Genji* as something that fits with his own Anglo-European tradition, indeed as a positive model to be adopted and adapted. It is no coincidence that this reading strongly resembles what continental authors such as Proust were publishing at the same time Waley was translating. His own opening lines, in a volume first published in 1925, read as follows:

> At the Court of an Emperor (he lived it matters not when) there was among the many gentlewomen of the Wardrobe and Chamber one, who though she was not of very high rank was favoured far beyond all the rest; so that the great ladies of the Palace, each of whom had secretly hoped that she herself would be chosen, looked with scorn and hatred upon the upstart who had dispelled their dreams. Still less were her former companions, the minor ladies of the Wardrobe, content to see her raised so far above them. Thus her position at Court, preponderant though it was, exposed her to constant jealousy and ill will; and soon, worn out with petty vexations, she fell into a decline, growing very melancholy and retiring frequently to her home. (Waley 1: 2)

Waley suggests that the historical dates of the purported Emperor are of no importance – we are reading literature after all – and finds equivalents for those problematic titles in borrowings from a European past by which he gently orients his readers. This is a court society, not so different from Camelot, perhaps, or Edwardian England. But let us pause for a moment to consider the rather stunning footnote appearing at the very beginning of this passage:

> This chapter should be read with indulgence. In it Murasaki, still under the influence of her somewhat childish predecessors, writes in a manner which is a blend of the Court chronicle with the conventional fairy-tale.

This prominent statement suggests that our translator does not quite have the courage of his convictions – a belief in the Genji's value to world literature that would paradoxically sustain him through the eight-year translation project. Although eager to have the work read in English, Waley is obviously concerned that his author will be dismissed as overly simplistic by an audience not sufficiently prepared for her work, and he thus effectively undermines her full acceptance.

The third generation of translators from Japanese to English appears in the 1960s and 1970s, when Japan and its culture have become more popularly known in the West and the *Genji* has begun to enjoy a broader general readership. The literature is now being presented in generally less exoticising or dismissive terms, although again this is not to say that the newer translations are more transparent or 'accurate' than the previous. Seidensticker, for all his improvement over Waley, still provides a subjective and heavily mediated reading. Here is his version of the passage in question:

> In a certain reign there was a lady not of the first rank whom the emperor loved more than any of the others. The grand ladies with high ambitions thought her a presumptuous upstart, and lesser ladies were still more resentful. Everything she did offended someone. Probably aware of what was happening, she fell seriously ill and came to spend more time at home than at court. The emperor's pity and affection quite passed bounds. No longer caring what his ladies and courtiers might say, he behaved as if intent upon stirring gossip. (Seidensticker 1976, 3)

As mentioned above, Seidensticker often reveals impatience with his author's languid, even labyrinthine sentence structure. Here we witness a typical chopping up of the Japanese text: Seidensticker has six sentences where each of the other translators stick more closely to the source text with only three. He also is the most terse, using no more than 93 words, where the ever-prolix Waley requires a total of 132 (for a difference of over 40 per cent; if we include Waley's footnote, which adds a further 35 words, the difference rises markedly to 80 per cent). An American with perhaps an inbred distrust of aristocratic pretensions, Seidensticker significantly downplays the regal setting of his text, opting to avoid upper case and to minimise the use of titles. Further, unlike his predecessors, who give pride of place to her lover the emperor, this translator chooses to make the woman the subject of the first sentence. This twist is, however, balanced by the fact that Seidensticker reveals the common sexist attitudes of his time with the derogatory gender-marked term 'gossip'.

A less widely known version of this passage is that published in Helen Craig McCullough's 1994 *Genji and Heike: Selections from* The Tale of Genji *and* The Tale of the Heike. This academic and translator conscientiously underscores the undeniable alterity of the world into which readers will be led, reminding us, for instance – in only the second sentence of her introduction – that the name by which we know our author is 'translatable as "purple ceremonial"' (3). McCullough is nonetheless intent on ensuring that her intended audience, primarily comprising 'students in survey courses and others who may lack the time to read [the tale] in [its] entirety' (ix), is grounded in the relevant historical and biographical facts that will equip them for a solid grasp of pre-modern Japanese culture. Her account of the Heian period is liberally sprinkled with dates and titles and, likewise, when she turns to this all-important opening scene of the narrative, we get a straightforward, no-nonsense reading:

> During the reign of a certain sovereign, it happened that one rather insignificant lady enjoyed far greater imperial favor than any of the other consorts and concubines. She was regarded with contempt and jealousy by proud ladies of superior status – personages who had always taken their own success very much for granted – and her equals and inferiors among the concubines felt even more disgruntled. Perpetually agitated by her constant presence at the emperor's side, her rivals made her bear an increasingly heavy burden of resentment. And whether for that reason or another, she grew frail and melancholy, and took to staying away from court. The emperor, who pitied her with all his heart, ignored the criticism and treated her in a manner that seemed destined to go down in history as an exemplar of favoritism. (25)

Note the long list of concrete nouns that make their appearance here, creating as clear as possible a sense of the particular setting or situation: 'consorts and concubines', 'contempt and jealousy', 'status', 'success', 'rivals', 'resentment', 'court', 'emperor', 'criticism', and so on, concluding with 'favoritism'. Even the term 'history' crops up – in a marked placement near the end of this first paragraph – suggesting that readers of this academic volume are encouraged to make use of the *Genji*'s fictional, literary world to help them understand Japan's real, documentable past. Further, a scholar's concern for thoroughness prompts her to be even more wordy than Waley, requiring a full 135 words to translate the passage.

Lastly, here is the most recent version of our text, crafted by Tyler at the turn of the twenty-first century:

> In a certain reign (whose can it have been?) someone of no very great rank, among all His Majesty's Consorts and Intimates, enjoyed exceptional favour. Those others who had always assumed that pride of place was properly theirs despised her as a dreadful woman, while the lesser Intimates were unhappier still. The way she waited on him day after day only stirred up feeling against her, and perhaps this growing burden of resentment was what affected her health and obliged her often to withdraw in misery to her home, but His Majesty, who could less and less do without her, ignored his critics until his behaviour seemed bound to be the talk of all. (3)

Tyler, publishing over 75 years after Waley and a full century after Suematsu, can safely assume his readership will possess some familiarity with this text, which has by now become fully canonised in both West and East. Accordingly, he is able to be more literal with the source than some of his predecessors, who had been obliged to make greater or lesser compromises in order to smooth the acceptance of very alien poetics. In other words, Tyler's explicitly or implicitly foreignising strategies make space for what Lawrence Venuti has famously championed as an 'ethics of difference' (see Venuti 1998).

Elements appearing here that closely reflect the Japanese original include the use of rhetorical questions interjected by the narrator, who delights in stepping out of the story on occasion and speaking directly to us; a strong tendency to vague or allusive expression; and an avoidance of any personal names. Given that many of these features remind us of Western postmodernism, we see how Tyler remains of his time even as he helps readers identify and understand that alternate focal point of the ellipsis. Unusual vocabulary or phrasing such as the reference to 'Consorts and Intimates' indicates a confidence that his present-day audience will be perfectly able to cope with strong hints of foreignness. Nonetheless, given the undeniable complexity and inherent difference of the text, Tyler (or his editor) still feels the need to provide extensive paratextual material such as a glossary, lists of characters, chapter summaries, time lines and so on. Indeed, the inclusion of this supplementary information helps position Tyler's translation as a coveted 'crossover book', reflecting the recent rise of publishers' interest in appealing to both a general readership as well as the specific market base of university classrooms.

These five translations, published across more than one hundred years, represent unique stages in the worlding of Japanese literature, offering the sensation of how this text has variously been read and put to use. Each affords us the opportunity to consider what it would mean to read as ourselves but also from a stance that is completely Other. The Japanese literary context may well be out of reach for those who have no access to its language or only limited access to its history and social constructions. Thus it is, through a critical reading of multiple translations as refractions, that we may find our way into that ellipse of comprehension, one that is rooted in and finds meaningful a text's radical cultural alterity. Whether or not it is true that the national always retains an 'ongoing, vital presence within the life of world literature' (Damrosch 284), in my view translation studies is uniquely located to identify and highlight how the national refracts successively, and not unproblematically, into the international.

Rewriting in a dominant language, as Casanova rightly states, is how the 'consecration' of foreign literature occurs: it is 'the principal means of access to the literary world for all writers outside the centre' (133). What I have sought to underscore is that this process is much more multilayered and less linear than either Casanova or Damrosch acknowledge, and that it is necessarily through a complex series of translative refractions – creative and idiosyncratic at their best – that world literature comes into being. It is worth bearing in mind that the Japanese terms for translation, 'hon'yaku' 翻訳, and adaptation, 'hon'an' 翻案, etymologically imply a 'turning' rather than the more common Western image of 'carrying across'. In an early version of this chapter, presented at the 2009 Nida School for Translation Studies in Italy, my subtitle was 'Turning Japanese' (in reference to a rather inane 1980s pop song), by which I intended to suggest that translation is indeed a process of turning and returning. Afterwards, postcolonial scholar Vicente Rafael pointed out that the accepted interpretation of the song lyrics is that they refer to male masturbation. Although this caused some mirth among those in attendance, the image could well be felicitous: these male scholars, titillated by the female-authored text, spilled their seed in the form of translations, from which have been somehow conceived further re-productions.

Through translation, Western literature and the other arts have become so influenced by this great masterpiece that they have to a degree themselves turned Japanese, incorporating aspects of the *Genji* at will. There is also that feedback loop mentioned earlier, whereby the Japanese have themselves been led to rethink their literary heritage based on how it has been received abroad. Translation studies scholars have of course long talked in terms of a cultural turn, a postcolonial turn or a sociological turn in our field. It should be clear by now that I see the specific 'turn' involved in both creating and reading literary translations as far from a simple, reductive one. It may be more of a Möbius strip than anything else, with the reader always simultaneously and somewhat confoundingly inside as well as outside the text.

Every translation, adaptation or imitation of the *Genji* represents one path that the complex original can take and, through these elliptical turnings, any traces of national origin obviously become 'increasingly diffused and... ever more sharply refracted as a work travels farther from home' (Damrosch 2003, 283). The well-travelled *Genji* has become something new; the translators take that resistance and turn the original Japanese into not only a series of English-language texts, but texts that clearly bear the marks of a very different locus, revealing that it can and does live on beyond its cultural origin. It is precisely in the range of possible readings, when juxtaposed with new contexts, that a given work finds its eligibility to enter a global canon. And foreign works must enter that canon through the idiosyncratic readings, even misreadings of translators, since these are what create the world literature text. By recognising that the multiplicity of interpretations and representations are 'not an unfortunate effect of our human limitations, [but rather] a semiotic necessity' (Stecconi 2009, 58), we can helpfully move beyond tired and restrictive conceptions of translation loss.

I am tempted to see the various *Genji Monogatari* that we now have in English, and all those that we presumably will have in the future, as part and parcel of the inherent multiplicity of those overlying tales so engagingly told by Murasaki Shikibu 1000 years ago and told again and anew in more recent times by her translators. In this light, it seems to me a lovely coincidence that Virginia Woolf, who wrote the first review of Waley's ultimately unreliable and yet rightly famed translation of the *Genji*, comments on viewing this foreign masterpiece 'through Mr Waley's beautiful telescope' (1967, 427).

A telescope presents the viewer with a brighter and clearer virtual image (and certain telescopes use refraction to accomplish this), despite offering merely one possible framing, and of course it will be a framing of what actually lies beyond our vision and what we may well misinterpret. The refractions discussed in this chapter help to demonstrate how translation functions as a prism that allows glimpses of many different and potential aspects of a complex work, according to what are necessarily differing understandings, aims and sensations. It is precisely through this process, these myriad refractive turns that an original takes as it encounters the intercultural interface upon successive retranslations, that the spectacular phenomenon of world literature gradually comes into focus.

References

Aston, W.G. 1897–98. 'The classical literature of Japan'. *Transactions and Proceedings of The Japan Society, London* IV: 274–285.

Casanova, Pascale. 2004. *The World Republic of Letters* [*La République mondiale des lettres*]. Trans. DeBevoise, M. B. Cambridge, Massachusetts: Harvard University Press.

Chamberlain, Basil Hall. 1890. *Things Japanese*. London: Kegan Paul.

Damrosch, David. 2003. *What Is World Literature?* Princeton and Oxford: Princeton University Press.

Edenbaum, Jane. '*The Tale of Genji* in living color: The Frankenthaler woodcuts.' PMA [Portland Museum of Art] Docent Research. January 2004. 1-2.

Henitiuk, Valerie. 2008. 'Going to bed with Waley: How Murasaki Shikibu does and does not become world literature'. *Comparative Literature Studies* 45(1): 40–61.

Lefevere, André. 2004. 'Mother Courage's cucumbers: Text, system and refraction in a theory of literature'. In *The Translation Studies Reader*. 2nd edn., edited by Venuti, Lawrence. New York and London: Routledge: 239–55.

Murasaki Shikibu. 1882. *Genji Monogatari*. Trans. Suyematz, Kenchio. London: Trübner & Co.

Murasaki Shikibu. 1925. *The Tale of Genji*. Trans. Waley, Arthur. London: George Allen & Unwin, Ltd.

Murasaki Shikibu. 1976. *The Tale of Genji*. Trans. Seidensticker, Edward. New York: Knopf.

Murasaki Shikibu. 1994. *Genji and Heike: Selections from* The Tale of Genji *and* The Tale of the Heike. Trans. McCullough, Helen Craig. Stanford, California: Stanford University Press.

Murasaki Shikibu. 2001. *The Tale of Genji*. Trans. Tyler, Royall. New York: Viking.

Stecconi, Ubaldo. 2009. 'What happens if we think that translating is a wave?' *Translation Studies* 3(1): 47–60.

Venuti, Lawrence. 1998. *The Scandals of Translation: Towards an Ethics of Difference*. London and New York: Routledge.

Woolf, Virginia. 1967. '*The Tale of Genji*. The first volume of Mr. Arthur Waley's translation of a great Japanese novel by the Lady Murasaki'. Rpt in *Literature East and West XL4*: 426–427.

Chapter 2

Leopoldo María Panero's per-versions

On translation considered as one of the fine arts

Ramón López Castellano

Por mi parte estoy convencido de que en cada época todos los poetas escriben, en distintas lenguas, el mismo poema. No hay un texto original, todos los textos son traducciones de ese poema que es, a su vez, una traducción. Y todos los lenguajes son traducciones de otro lenguaje, que es también una traducción.

(Octavio Paz)

El sueño de Peter Pan no es dulce y la literatura de L. Carroll da miedo.

(Leopoldo María Panero)

Leopoldo María Panero is possibly one of the most renowned living Spanish poets. After a lengthy and extreme literary career Panero has perfected an inimitable poetic voice, which has earned him general respect and admiration by critics and readers alike and has given him cult status. Due to his hazardous biography and radical literary practices, Panero also has the doubtful honour of being the official *poète maudit* of Spanish letters. Both his overwhelming poetic persona and the imposing force of his original writings have entirely overshadowed his labour as a literary translator and translation theorist. In the following pages I shed some light on Panero's novel theory and practices of translation, which may well constitute the most radical praxes ever to have been witnessed in Spanish literature, and which testify to the understanding of translation as a purely creative and 'original' literary mode.

In his early production, Panero's poetic work alternates with his labour as a literary translator. The young poet commenced his career in translation with *El ómnibus sin sentido* (1972). This bilingual edition of Edward Lear's limericks was released when Panero had published only one book, *Así se fundó Carnaby Street* (1970). In 1975 a new translation of various obscure Lewis Carroll texts was published as a collection entitled *Matemática demente*. In the prose volume, *El lugar del hijo* (1976), the stories 'Medea' and 'La visión' are adaptations of Fitz James O'Brien's short stories. One year later, in *Visión de la literatura de terror anglo-americana*, Panero selected and translated a few horror stories by 'peripheral' Anglo-American authors (including Clark Ashton Smith and Vernon Lee) and Robert Browning's 'Childe Roland to the Dark Tower Came'. It could be argued that, at least in a quantitative way, in the first ten years of his career Panero's work as a translator eclipsed his poetic production. A further translation appeared in 1982, *La caza del Snark, paroxismo en ocho espasmos*, another version of Lewis Carroll's *The Hunting of the Snark* (1874). In 1984 Panero adapted Arthur Machen's 'The Inmost Light' as 'La luz inmóvil' in the prose book *Dos relatos y una perversión*. Finally, the translation of J. M. Barrie's novel, *Peter and Wendy*, appeared in the late 1980s. It purported to be by Panero and became his most renowned and celebrated translation. After this publication, the poet's enthusiasm for translation seemed to fade.

Panero's idiosyncratic practice of translation has often been accompanied by heavy and sophisticated theorisation in the prologues and prefaces that appear in most of his adaptations of foreign – mostly English-speaking – authors' works.[1] Theory and practice seem to work concurrently towards the realisation of an ultimate effect: the *perversion* of the 'original'. In the following pages I discuss the radical evolution of Panero's distinctive modes of translation together with the possible effects and repercussions that these practices may have for the understanding not only of literary translation, but also of the literary in a broader sense.

---

1   The reason Panero has circumscribed his translations to English texts remains a mystery. As can be seen throughout his oeuvre, the poet possesses a solid knowledge of at least Latin, French, Italian and German.

Translation

Much has been made in contemporary theory of the impossibility of literary translation. In one of her introductions to the topic Susan Bassnett quotes Roman Jakobson's claim that 'Both the theory and the practice of translation abound with intricacies, from time to time attempts are made to sever the Gordian knot by proclaiming the dogma of untranslatability' (Bassnett 1991, 135). Bassnett states that despite some authors incessantly bemoaning the impossibility of translation, 'translators continue to translate' (1991, 135). Over the past forty years the field of translation theory has undergone a series of critical advances, following a parallel track with developments in philosophy in general, and theory of literature and linguistics in particular. These changes, as is well known, chiefly entail a mutation of the notion of Text, which ceases to be a well-established, self-referential and iconic entity and becomes an unstable, contradictory, relative, open image, created and re-created by and within the complex networks of discourse. Therefore, what was formerly a 'clear' equation of source text = target text has been vastly problematised. This theoretical and practical shift is embodied by many translators' approval of the model of 'free translation'. The acknowledgment of the entelechy involved in the idea of a literal translation leads theorists to agree – to some extent – that translation entails the creation of metaphorical or allegorical versions, the free choice of interpretation, and a certain degree of co-authorship.

The awareness of the contemporary complexities and dilemmas posed by translation surfaces very early on in Panero's career. In fact, the poet takes theoretical and practical sides in a rather drastic way. In the prologue to *El ómnibus sin sentido*, entitled 'Lo que por fin dijo Benjamin', Panero confirms his status as *agent provocateur* by challenging the question of untranslatability in quite a dismissive way: 'good' poetry is complex and open to '*infinitos desarrollos*' (1972, 7; 'infinite developments'), and as such, it demands to be translated. The claims about the impossibility of translation are mere '*frasecitas imbéciles*' (1972, 7; 'idiodic commonplaces'). In this sense he seems to follow closely Walter Benjamin's notion of translatability, the 'essential quality of certain works', by which 'a specific significance inherent in the original manifests itself in the translation' (Benjamin 1969, 71). Nevertheless, from the very beginning Panero regards translation in a rather peculiar way. In the essay, the poet offers a clear set of four maxims about the nature and the goals of his adaptations:

> *Que a la traducción cumple desarrollar –o superar– el original y no trasladarlo...*
> *Que la labor del poeta es tan primitiva y la del traductor, en cambio, reflexiva,*

'ideal', no dejándose llevar por la bestia de la intuición. Que traducción y traducido no deben ser paralelas, sino una tangente (la traducción) que toca el círculo (lo traducido). Que, en fin, es deber de la traducción hacer de lo que simboliza lo simbolizado: invertirlo todo como el poeta ha hecho. (1972, 7)

Translation must develop – or exceed – the original, not transfer it... The poet's task is primitive, while the translator's task is reflexive and 'ideal', never carried away by the beast of intuition. Translation and translated should never be parallel texts, but a tangent (the translation) touching a circle (the translated). Finally, the duty of translation is to turn what it symbolises into the symbolised: to invert everything as the poet has previously done.

The first principle, that of translation as developing and superseding the original, is related to the notions of correction, plagiarism and explanation. In the prologue to *Dos relatos y una perversión* Panero claims '*corrijo más que traduzco*' (1984, 12; 'I correct more than I translate'). The poet's notion of linguistic transposition as correction is obviously not an innovative proposal. Gerard Genette, for instance, quotes Louis Aragon's conception of his hypertextual practices – like those of Lautréamont – as corrections of the 'originals' (Genette 1997, 360). Yet this idea of the correction of the source text needs some clarification. In contemporary theoretical accounts of textuality, as well as in Panero's practices as a poet himself, literature offers no room for originality as an absolute category. Panero's Borgesian claim that '*toda la literatura no es sino una inmensa prueba de imprenta y nosotros, los escritores últimos o póstumos, somos tan sólo correctores de pruebas*' (1984, 12; 'all literature is nothing but an immense galley proof and we, the latest or posthumous writers, are but its proof readers') precludes the possibility of both originality and authorship *strictu sensu*. Regarding the riddle of originality as applied to translation, Octavio Paz, a conspicuous translator and theorist himself, claimed, rather unexceptionably, that:

> *en un extremo el mundo se nos presenta como una colección de heterogeneidades; en el otro, como una superposición de textos, cada uno ligeramente distinto al anterior: traducción de traducciones de traducciones, cada texto es único y, simultáneamente, es la traducción de otro texto.* (1981, 8)

on the one hand, the world is presented to us as a collection of heterogeneities; on the other, as a textual superimposition, each text subtly different from the previous one: translation of translations of translations, every text is unique, yet, simultaneously, it is the translation of another text.

In the endless and relational world of textuality the only possibility offered to the reader entails the acceptance of the relentless flow of signs and the constant displacement of signifiers. Within this context originality constitutes a free signifier that can be assigned to every text and to none. The translator, Panero, has received multiple criticisms relating to his supposed lack of fidelity to the source texts, as his self-defence in the prologue to *Matemática* testifies.[2] These accusations within our – and his – present theoretical framework are merely out of place. Graciela Isnardi, praising Paz's translations, comments that '*la combinación de imaginación y fidelidad [es] lo que hace que ante un traductor de la categoría de Octavio Paz, el viejo e irónico* traduttore, tradittore *se transforme en* traduttore, creatore' (1979, 730–31; '[it is] the combination of imagination and fidelity which enables Octavio Paz, the translator, to turn the old and ironical *traduttore, tradittore* into *traduttore, creatore*'). In Panero, however, the question cannot revolve around the dilemma between *traditore* and *creatore*. Roman Jakobson, in his essay 'On Linguistic Aspects of Translation', claims:

> If we were to translate into English the traditional formula *Traduttore, traditore* as 'the translator is a betrayer,' we would deprive the Italian rhyming epigram of all its paronomastic value. Hence a cognitive attitude would compel us to change this aphorism into a more explicit statement and to answer the questions: translator of what messages? betrayer of what values? (2006, 335)

Within a theoretical and practical framework that enacts the absence of the possibility of imagination or fidelity and the absence of univocal messages and assured values,[3] the issue that concerns us should not be directly related to old Byzantine discussions about originality or fidelity. Rather, the discussion should aim to ascertain how Panero's translations work and what effects they may produce as literary phenomena.[4]

---

2   Panero's short essay that opens the volume, 'Olvidar: esa venganza' (Carroll 1975, 9–14), is a diatribe against several criticisms incurred by his translation of Lear in *El ómnibus sin sentido*.

3   For a discussion of Panero's oeuvre as a palimpsestic set of writings that challenge interpretation and authorship see Chapter V in López Castellano (2010).

4   When I refer to the workings and effects of Panero's translations I am loosely subscribing to a Deleuzian theoretical framework. Deleuze has been a constant inspiration for Panero,

In Panero's early principles of translation, once originality as an absolute category is rejected, the related and paradoxical notion of correction can be better understood in terms of plagiarism and explanation. Regarding plagiarism, Lautréamont, one of Panero's most admired authors, claimed that '*Le plagiat est nécessaire. Le progrès l'implique. Il* serre de près *la phrase d'un auteur, se sert de ses expressions,* efface *une idée fausse, la remplace par l'idée juste*' (1992, 259; 'Plagiarism is necessary. Progress implies it. It holds an author's phrase, uses his expressions, erases a false idea and replaces it with the right idea'). Plagiarism is, therefore, not a flaw of the literary work. It actually constitutes an inherent form, a connatural act implied in the progression of literature – understood in the present reading as mere expansion, not teleological progress. *Plagium* in Latin means 'a kidnapping', the violent removal of a being into a different place. The plagiarism involved in translation entails a removal of the text to a new language, and to a new sociocultural space. In this process the form of the 'original' is lost, as is its 'original' potential reader. The original's 'wrong idea' is effaced by translation and substituted by the 'right one' in Lautréamont's words. Within a contemporary textual framework, however, right and wrong cannot be regarded as ethical or aesthetic categories. They may be understood in this context as mere functions of the flow of progression of the literary – conceived of as sheer movement, in a non-positivist way. It is in this sense that we can appreciate the meaning of translation as explanation. As Panero states, the translated text develops '*los sentidos latentes en el original explicándolo (lo que en latín significa desplegarlo)*' (1975, 11; 'the meanings that are latent in the original, explaining them (which in Latin means displacing them)'). Indeed, explaining relates to a process of unfolding; that is, expanding the text, using the 'original' to create and re-create in an endless textual increase. Translation thus conceived differs in no way from any other form of literary re-writing – that is, writing. In this respect Panero, referring once more to Lautréamont, states that '*la literatura... otorga a la cita, a la lectura y a la traducción el máximo valor, como los más arriesgados exponentes de la naturaleza sistemática de la literatura. Y considera a la traducción lo mismo que a la cita y a la lectura como lo que son, reescrituras*' (1977, 29–30; 'literature... gives quoting, reading and translating the same status as the riskiest exponents of the systematic nature of literature. It regards translation, quoting and reading as what they actually are, rewritings').

Reading seems to be the primary concern in Panero's second principle of translation, which involves the contrast between the task of the poet and that

---

not only in his theory essays and poetry, but also in his translations. The Deleuzian theoretical framework will be briefly expanded upon later in this chapter.

of the translator. The former is meant to be primitive and intuitive whereas the later is characterised as reflexive and 'ideal'. Nonetheless, this assertion may entail a great deal of naivety. Firstly, Panero constantly states in his writings the obvious fact exposed by late twentieth-century developments on the theorisation of the literary – and of the author – that textuality precludes pure intuition. Secondly, Panero himself has often proven to be utterly aware of the 'rational', or the structural and technical, nature of his own writing as a poet. Despite acknowledging a certain level of intuitive 'surrealism' in his first book, *Así se fundó Carnaby Street*, Panero declared a departure from the non-reflexive, the irrational and the inspired very early on in his literary career (1971, 18). The poet has proclaimed on several occasions his adherence to '*la poesía técnicamente bien escrita... la del propio Mallarmé*' (Panero 2001b; 'poetry well written from a technical point of view... like Mallarmé's'), while rejecting the intuitive elements involved in innocent, conversational, or even surrealist poetic practices.

If there is no 'creative' ground for the distinction between the task of the writer and that of the translator, the question is whether such a distinction exists at all and, if it does, whether it has any impact on the translated work. Panero's discussion of the reflexive and ideal work of the translator is primarily based upon the act of reading. The poet has stated that '*toda obra está abierta a cualquier lectura, toda obra es una Grieta para la que cabe cualquier interpretación: y sólo por ello es posible la traducción*' (1975, 11; 'every piece is open to any reading, every piece is a Crack in which any interpretation fits: it is this Crack and nothing else that makes translation possible'). Subsequently, reading is the activity that locates in the original the 'cracks' through which the infinite possibility of meaning leaks and expands. Therefore only reading makes translation possible by actualising the ongoing translatability of the text.[5] The cracks, found and opened by reading, are the tangential relationship and the fluid nexus that Panero posits in his third maxim. Octavio Paz, in *El signo y el garabato*, discusses the similarity of the translator's activity and that of the reader and the critic. Every reading is a translation and every critique is an interpretation (Paz 1973, 66). Therefore, in Panero's theory, translation seems to constitute a privileged medium for the fluid transmission of the

---

5   Derrida makes the expected connection between translatability and ongoing readability (the 'life' of the text, which in turn could be paralleled to its writeability in Barthesian terms): 'A text lives only if it lives on, and it lives on only if it is at once translatable and untranslatable... Totally translatable, it disappears as a text, as writing, as a body of language. Totally untranslatable, even within what is believed to be one language, it dies immediately' (1999, 102).

multiple signifying potential of textual communication, notwithstanding the impossibility of a 'Meaning'.

According to Panero's fourth maxim of translation, the procedure of reading involved in linguistic transposition has a singular goal, that is, to make what symbolises the symbolised in a process of inversion, as the poet has previously done (1972, 7). Paz states that the specificity of the translator's reading and re-writing arises from the fact that his point of departure is fixed. The source text is 'frozen' language, yet alive, translatable. The translator's task, then, is inverse to that of the poet. In a similar way to Panero, Paz claims '*No se trata de construir con signos móviles un texto inamovible, sino desmontar los elementos de ese texto, poner de nuevo en circulación los signos y devolverlos al lenguaje*' (1973, 66; 'the issue is not to construct a fixed text with mobile signs, but to dismantle the elements in the text and put the signs in circulation again, thus taking them back to language'). From the very beginning, however, the translator confronts the source text knowing that the final result must be an analogous product cast in a new language. This restriction, according to Paz, constitutes the key difference between the work of the poet and the task of the translator. Nevertheless, the inversion produced by the translator is never a copy, but a transmutation of the 'original' (Paz 1973, 66). Translation thus understood is more a hermeneutic art than a linguistic operation, an art consisting of finding and constructing analogies and correspondences, '*un arte de sombras y ecos*' (Paz 1973, 66; 'an art of shadows and echoes').

Therefore there seems to be a fundamental limitation and distinction here between the work of the translator and that of the poet. This limitation, apparently supported by the theories of both Panero and Paz, is related to the need for an analogy between source and target texts, and as such is a purely hermeneutical distinction.

Taking into account the central notion of analogy, what kind of translator, then, is Panero, the poet-translator? Two samples of his first translations provide an answer to this question. *El ómnibus sin sentido*, Panero's bilingual collection of Edward Lear's limericks, opens with the following poem:

There was an Old Person of Chili,

Whose conduct was painful and silly;

He sat on the stairs

Eating apples and pears,

That imprudent Old Person of Chili. (1972, 14)

On the following page Panero's translation renders:

Erase en tiempos un viejo en Chili

Cuya conducta fue estúpida y penosa;

Sentado en las escaleras

Comió manzanas y peras

Este imprudente viejo de Chili. (1972, 15)

Túa Blesa has claimed that '*en esta primera incursión nuestro poeta no se concedió los márgenes de libertad que más adelante invadiría*' (1995, 80; 'in this first translation our poet did not give himself the liberty he would take later on'). The poet, indeed, offers the Spanish reader a rather orthodox and 'canonical' transposition of the original. It is important to note, however, that Panero adapts Lear's *A Book of Nonsense* to initiate his translation practice. The tradition of *nonsense*, indeed, represents an ideal ground for translation, since, in the writings it comprises, 'meaning' is often subservient to humour, pun and the playfulness of the absurd. Therefore, for the translation practice, the concerns with the entelechy of the faithful transposition of meaning can be downplayed in favour of the formal aspects of linguistic conversion. As seen in this first limerick, this conversion is carried out in a somewhat accurate manner, despite certain questionable decisions in terms of linguistic precision.[6] In this transposition, the traditional toponym that finishes Lear's first lines, 'Chili', which actually does not designate any real city or country in either English or Spanish – although it carries the obvious resonance of both Chile and chilli – is kept in its original form. Rhythm and rhyme, traditional 'nemeses' of the translator, are also transported from the source to the target text. Not only the obvious transposition of the rhyme in Chili in the first and last lines, but also 'stairs' and 'pears' keep their phonetic consonance in '*escaleras*' and '*peras*'. Therefore this translation appears to challenge Panero's own theory discussed above. The new poem, indeed, does not seem to be a very productive attempt to supersede the original, to develop it, or to open a tangential relationship between both texts.

---

6   Of these, probably the most remarkable is the verbal tense chosen in the translation: In terms of 'faithfulness' Spanish imperfect preterite would have been much more appropriate than the indefinite preterite.

Several other translations in *El Ómnibus*, however, seem to regard translation as a more adventurous enterprise and, as such, they follow Panero's own radical principles more closely. The limits of the notion of analogy seem to be explored in a more eager fashion in other poems of which the following is a clear example:

There was an Old Person of Minety,

Who purchased five hundred and ninety

Large apples and pears,

Which he threw unawares,

At the heads of the people of Minety. (1972, 72)

Hubo una vez un viejo en Noventa

Que compró exactamente trescientas

Manzanas y peras de aire

Las que arrojó sin que se dieran cuenta

Sobre las cabezas del pueblo de Noventa. (1972, 73)

In this translation the limerick's geographic reference comprises the first 'anomaly'. Minety, the name of a small English provincial town – probably chosen by Lear for its phonic resemblance with ninety – is interpreted and translated by Panero as '*Noventa*'. The 'original' *topos* of the poem becomes a non-place, an impossible location. Most importantly, the number in line two in the original, 'five hundred and ninety' is translated, in a totally unmotivated way, by '*exactamente trescientas*' ('exactly three hundred'). This procedure perfectly exemplifies the translator's reading and re-writing as pure creation. The number in the source text offers no possibility of fixed meaning, if we understand meaning in terms of symbolic interpretation. It is a perfect instance of *nonsense*, the crack in the text where sense both disappears and becomes multiple sense. Confronted with the purely – and improbable – face value of the number, the translator replaces it in a totally nonsensical manner. The chosen number does not even respect the consonant rhyme the original had created between 'Minety' and 'ninety' – which would have been rather an easy turn, taking into account that 40, 50, 60, 70 and 80 rhyme with '*Noventa*' in Spanish. Therefore, the translation '*trescientas*' stands as nonsense of the *nonsense*, nonsense in the second degree.

Furthermore, the lack of logicality and the 'meaninglessness' of the original number and its Spanish counterpart are enhanced by the introduction of the adverb '*exactamente*', absent in the source text. Thus numbers, these actual cracks in meaning, become focused and reinforced as (non)*sense*, that is, as the locus for meaning to flow, to spill or escape and proliferate. There *must* be some meaning to a number, if the Old Man inhabits a place called 'Noventa', the translation seems to say. But not only that, the adverb introduced in the translation points at an 'exact' number: the translator's choice is then presented as precise and 'motivated' by an impossible 'truth' of meaningful, allegorical meaning that is supposed to sit either behind the poem or within the poem's logic. '*Exactamente*' generates a kind of trap that illuminates with its semantic focus what is, in fact, the actual crack in meaning of the text, which in turn activates the proliferation of the literary. In this sense, Panero's claim in his prologue that the translation must supersede, expand and, in a way, 'correct' the original acquires full meaning (1972, 7).

Two additional elements in the text exemplify Panero's early departure from the understanding of translation as purely analogous and his new perception of it as a fundamentally creative device. The translation of 'Large apples and pears' as '*Manzanas y peras de aire*' not only denotes a significant departure from the original, but also indicates the introduction of a thoroughly anachronistic literary trace. Paz has argued that a translator should have the capacity to participate in both the language system of the original and its world view, and that, without this capacity, he or she will not be able to translate in a meaningful way (Paz 1985, 159). Against this extended belief Panero introduces a purely – and suspiciously obvious – surrealistic image. Regardless of the surrealists' appreciation of Lear, it is evident that the creator of the limericks wrote within a previous 'world view' to the beginning of the historical Avant-Gardes. The insertion of this image in 'Lear's' text translated into Spanish makes it not 'his' anymore, but a contemporary text, an independent creation by a contemporary voice. This re-appropriation is finally enhanced in the last line of the translation, which clearly introduces a sample of Panero's typical imagery by a subtle linguistic turn. '*Sobre las cabezas del pueblo*' could be regarded a faithful linguistic transposition of 'At the heads of the people'. Nevertheless, the choice '*pueblo*' – one of the possible equivalents for 'people' in Spanish – instead of '*gente*' (which may have been the most obvious first choice) creates a disturbing image. In fact, the syntagm '*cabezas del pueblo*' can be read as 'the heads of the people' but also as 'the heads of the village' and even 'the heads owned by the village'. This objectification of the head – and the decapitated head – is a typical and recurrent image in Panero's texts.[7]

These samples of Panero's first adaptations clearly show his conception of the translator's task as rewriting and recreation, despite some inconsistency and contention regarding the radical practical implications of the concept. Translation is a reflexive activity that develops and may even 'exceed' the original and it generates a tangential relationship with the source text by creating a (relatively) analogous literary artefact in a different language. In spite of the fact that huge difficulties are involved in literary translation, the linguistic transposition of the literary text is not only possible, but also utterly legitimate. The task of the translator may be almost indistinguishable from that of the poet, as Paz writes: '*los poetas de lengua inglesa, en particular Eliot y Pound, han mostrado que la traducción es una operación indistinguible de la creación poética*' (1973, 135; 'English-language poets, particularly Eliot and Pound, have proven that translation is an operation indistinguishable from poetic creation'). Nevertheless, due to the need for a certain degree of analogy, translation may be a kind of game in which inventiveness interplays with fidelity: '*el traductor no tiene más remedio que inventar el poema que imita*' (Paz 1979, 12; 'the translator has no choice but to invent the poem he imitates'). In Panero's first translating praxis, however, some unsettling features appear that may eventually challenge and overflow this theoretical framework in which 'imitation' is still an issue. These features will leave the door open to the next stage, that of translation as perversion.

Per-version

Panero's theories were further developed in *Matemática demente*, his selection and translation of some obscure Lewis Carroll texts. Panero's lengthy preface to the volume seems to 'adapt' Gilles Deleuze's heavily Carrollian *Logique du sens* – to which the poet refers with the 'hallucinogenic' pun '*L.S.D. (Lógica del sentido)*' (1975, 42; 'LSD (Logic of sense)'). It is in this preface that Panero introduces his notion of '*per-versión*'. This concept may

---

7   In his analysis of 'Ma mère' Medina refers to headlessness as a recurrent topic in Panero, '*una escena recurrente a lo largo de su poesía: la muerte y desintegración del yo se visualiza con una cabeza abierta y mutilada*' (Medina 2001, 163; 'a recurrent scene throughout his poetry: the death and integration of the self is represented with an open, mutilated head').

actually be a playful 'per-version' of Octavio Paz's theories of translation as exposed in his book *Versiones y diversiones*, in which Paz adapted texts by some of the authors who have been most influential in Panero's poetry, including Donne, Pound, Cummings, Crane, Nerval and Mallarmé. In this volume, he states that he aimed at writing poems in his own language, taking as a point of departure other poems in other languages (Paz 1975, 9). Therefore, translation is still understood by Paz as a process of re-writing linked to a recognisable source.

Yet rewriting necessarily entails a 'manipulation' and an inescapable per-version of the original. Panero's 'second stage' as translator appears to explore this 'perverse' aspect of translation in an exceptionally eager way. The third sense of '*glosar*' in the *Diccionario de la Real Academia Española* defines the action of glossing as a sinister and biased interpretation – a meaning that is also found in the archaic English forms 'gloss on' and 'gloss upon'. This specific meaning presupposes the fact that the act of reading and rewriting opens the locus for perversion, the 'disturbing' and 'unfaithful' interpretation of the vulnerable 'original'. This idea has been regarded as common knowledge from the very beginning of literacy – hence, for example, Plato's severe suspicions concerning writing and Derrida's subsequent overturn of Plato in 'Plato's Pharmacy'. As an eager reader of Derrida, Panero's notion of per-version plays on the indeterminacy of rewriting. Despite embracing the inherent sinister side of the process, the poet's idea seems to be also concerned with other usages and meanings of the word. The hyphenated prefix 'per' denotes in Spanish not only negativity but, most importantly for our discussion, intensity or totality. Furthermore, the Latin origin of perversion, *pervertĕre*, means 'to turn about', to move so that what is moved faces in the opposite direction. Likewise, Panero's per-version could be defined as literary turnabout in search of intensity, indicating a (multiple) totality, sometimes with possible sinister effects.

The preface to *Matemática demente* opens with a delightful diatribe against the criticisms which Panero's '*versión de Lear*' (Panero 1972, 9) had attracted due to its adventurousness and, in the critics' opinion, its intolerable unfaithfulness. In the text, entitled 'Olvidar: esa venganza' (1972, 9–14), a haughtily magnanimous Panero condemns his critics to oblivion and not only reaffirms his ideas on translation, but threatens the reader with the new concept of '*perversión*' (1972, 9). After proclaiming the death of the author the poet goes on to reclaim the dimension of translation as a purely creative and literary task: '... *la traducción, que hasta hoy ha sido considerada como una labor anónima y humilde... es –o debe ser– por contrario una operación literaria, creadora, si es que lo traducido es literatura y si se quiere, efectivamente, traducirlo'* (1972, 15; '... translation, often regarded as an anonymous and humble task... is, or should be, a literary and creative operation, if what is being translated is actual literature and if one wants to actually translate it'). The idea of translation as development and correction of the original is further expanded. Panero quotes Deleuze in *Logic of Sense*: '... *cada nombre que designa el sentido de otro anterior es de un grado superior a ese nombre y a lo que designa'* (Panero 1972, 14; 'every noun that designates the sense of a former one is a degree superior to that noun and what it designates'). Therefore, the act of reading and rewriting – interpretation – involved in translation entails a proliferative and transformational process of re-signification, which, in turn, opens itself to new developments. The mode of 'explanation', of which translation becomes a conspicuous paradigm, does not circumscribe sense; on the contrary, it empowers it. If literature is the production of sense, translation becomes the second degree of literature. This heavily Deleuzian theoretical framework was further developed by Panero in later publications:

> *Más que interpretar conviene así desenrollar la obra de arte: transformar ese sentido en una significación que sólo puede ser como cualquier sentido significado, como cualquier efecto de una terrible boda, destructora, revolucionaria. Explicatio (desenvolvimiento), no interpretación. La explicatio no castra el sentido por el significado, sino que hace a este doblemente potente, dotándole de significación, de LSD o de lógica del sentido.* (Panero 1998, 165)

More than interpretation, an unfolding of the work of art is required: to transform sense in a mode of signification that can only be like any signified sense, like the effect of a terrible, destructive and revolutionary marriage. Explicatio (unfolding), not interpretation. Explicatio does not emasculate sense to create meaning, on the contrary, it empowers sense by giving it signification, LSD, or the logic of sense.

In translation, however, *explicatio* as unfolding of signification always involves absolute degree of undecidability; it is a liminal act of faith that confronts the impossibility of meaning. Aware of its own liminality, per-version is a risky operation that both destroys and recreates the 'original' and the 'translation'. In Panero's words, per-version unfolds '*a costa de ambos, cuando el sentido per-vierta a la letra, y la letra al sentido*' (1975, 17; 'at the expense of both, when meaning per-verts expression and expression per-verts meaning'). The procedure attempts a synthesis of form and sense, and sense and meaning, that is, the marriage of 'contraries'. Panero is conscious of the entelechy involved in the *coincidentia oppositorum* – when opposites coincide without ceasing to be themselves – but translation is an impossibility that has to be attempted. The poet appeals to the heuristic – and, of course, profoundly questionable – capacities of alchemy, defined as '*la unión de lo que no puede unirse*' (1975, 16; 'the union of what cannot be united'), which can produce the miracle of the actual development of senses and contents that were embryonic in the original, that is, '*los contenidos latentes*' (1975, 17; 'the latent contents'). The translator's faith in his method is such that he dares to claim that '*La per-versión es pues, la única traducción literal, o mejor dicho, fiel al original: y esto lo logra mediante un adulterio, mediante su –aparente– infidelidad*' (Panero 1975, 17; 'Per-version is the only literal translation. Its true faithfulness to the original is achieved by an adultery, through its apparent infidelity').

Yet in Panero's theoretical development of per-version, the notion of the analogy between the original and the translation is still kept as a core principle:

> … *para 'producir', con medios diferentes, efectos análogos… la Per-versión no dudará en añadir, si es preciso, palabras, versos enteros, párrafos enteros para así dejar intacto el Sentido del original y hacer que la traducción de éste produzca en el lector el mismo efecto estético que le produciría la lectura del original.* (1975, 17–18)

> … in order to produce analogous effects with different means… per-version will not hesitate to add, if needed, words, full lines or paragraphs so that the original Sense remains intact and the translation creates the same aesthetic effect in the reader as would be produced by reading the original.

This paragraph, imbued with a certain degree of naivety, discusses both the technique and the effects of per-version. However, Panero's subsequent practice of translation will challenge the core of its theoretical presuppositions – and the common understanding of translation: analogy. A most revealing instance of this can be provided by an analysis of his translation of Carroll's *The Hunting of the Snark* (1874).

La caza del Snark (1982) was Panero's last book entirely devoted to translation. Per-version now seems to acquire full potential and becomes an all-encompassing destructive/creative force growing in a chaotic and untamed way, even to the point of confronting its own theoretical origins. The comprehensive per-version in the book begins even before the translated text makes its appearance: indeed, in the preface, Panero makes 'his' Carroll discuss '*la nefanda y perversa intención de traducir. Porque traducir es pervertir, es, de algún modo, crear monstruos*' (1982, 8; 'the nefarious and perverse intention behind translation. Because translating is perverting, a mode of monster creation'), a remark absent in the original. In order to analyse one of the horde of 'monsters' that populate this volume, the first lines of Carroll's pinnacle of *nonsense* are quoted below and followed by Panero's perversion. 'Unmotivated' additions in the translation are underlined.

FIT THE FIRST

THE LANDING

'Just the place for a Snark!' the Bellman cried,
As he landed his crew with care;
Supporting each man on the top of the tide
By a finger entwined in his hair.

'Just the place for a Snark! I have said it twice:
That alone should encourage the crew.
Just the place for a Snark! I have said it thrice:
What I tell you three times is true' (Carroll 1998, 680)

PRIMER ESPASMO

El desembarco

Aquí el agua llora; aquí mi rostro

encuentra su velo, y el can

no puede lamerme: '*Éste es*

el mejor sitio para un Snark' eso dijo el Hombre

de la Campana, amenazando al lector con el puño

antes de mostrar la sangre: y puso en tierra

a toda su tripulación con ternura

pasándolos por encima de la ola

con el dedo perdido en sus cabellos:

'Aquí no llora el mar: éste es el sitio

Aquí no llora el mar: éste es mi rostro.

Éste es el sitio, éste es el aroma del Snark,

estas palabras lo llaman, moviendo la cola frágilmente,

la cabeza bajando y subiendo los ojos para en ellos

no mirar: ésta es la guarida, dos veces lo dije,

en que el Snark se desnuda, incitando a la cópula

a todos los otros Snarks: –también nosotros

gemimos por el sexo del Snark– éste es el sitio húmedo

ya tres y cuatro veces lo dije, y cinco lo diré sin duda

y lo que digo cinco veces es verdad' (Carroll 1982, 12)

At first sight, it seems rather evident that prudishness and containment are cast aside in this per-version. Leaving aside the obvious obliteration of the musicality and the rhyme in the original, what surprises the reader is the drastic increase in the poem's materiality: eight lines in the original become twenty in the adaptation. What appeared in former translations as a more or less subtle expansion has become an explosion. Túa Blesa, when commenting on this translation, uses the term *amplificatio* (1995, 88) to refer to its technique. *Amplificatio*, though, is not the only site of the per-version. Indeed, the perverse transposition carried out in this poem affects both the 'new' lines that proliferate in an ostensibly unbridled way and the lines that could be regarded as 'analogous' to the original. Thus, the translation of lines 2–4 in the original may be perceived as 'unfaithful' and, as such, already a re-creation of latent contents. Most importantly, the three identical 'Just the place for a Snark!' in the original are not only rendered by four scattered and broken translations, but the possibility of a fifth is opened by the penultimate line of the per-version. This proliferation no longer responds to any explanation as 'meaningful' device, but to mere excess, the overflow of signs that float in the text's tide without an anchor to any possible core meaning. Analogy is no longer a feasible justification for the three lines that open the poem. Before the first line of 'The Landing' there is nothing, only the vacuum of the blank page, silence. With this emptiness, the per-version begets three monstrous lines, three lines without an 'original' author that, in turn, provide the poem with an 'authorial' narrator's voice in the first grammatical person. This voice metaphorically conveys the veiling of the alleged author's voice, trapping authority in a labyrinth of mirrors, and precluding the possibility of an authoritarian presence in a way which is exceedingly characteristic of Panero's poetry. In Panero's lines 5–6 the 'Hombre de la Campana', that caring Bellman in the original, threatens the reader with his fist before showing him blood; yet again the translation incorporates two completely unmotivated lines, two passages that Panero finds and that open in the core of the *nonsensic* original, paradoxically, in order to let sense spill, escape and proliferate in a liminal sea of uncertainty and impossibility. Hence, perhaps, the ominous threat of the new Bellman; maybe his threat is trying to protect the reader from the dangers of per-version, the translation that opens the gate of the multiple, the absolute uncertainty that lurks behind the open gates of (a)signification.[8]

The *amplificatio* in lines 12–18 is equally 'unmotivated' by the original. The translator simply reads, interprets and creates. He fills the crack that he finds in the original with a completely new text that only vaguely resembles its alleged source by mentioning the Snark. Panero's Snark, however, is a dark and lascivious creature that incites the universe – other snarks, the sailors, the reader – to the copula. The Snark is a monster that mirrors the monstrous nature of the per-version. Discussing Carroll's creature, Deleuze argues '"Snark" is an unheard-of name, but it is also an invisible monster. It refers to a formidable action, the hunt, at the end of which the hunter is dissipated and loses his identity' (1990, 67). Panero's empowered Snark is both hunter and prey, the monster made of disjointed and opposed limbs, the shadow of unrecognisable form that signals the point where the contraries cannot be united. Yet, as an alchemist, the Snark bridges the gap with(in) the endless possibility of meaning, generating a sort of 'fourth' dimension of meaning, that is, sense. This sense signals the vacuum within itself and, conversely, the endless multiplicity of infinitude. As Deleuze claims, 'In truth, the attempt to make this fourth dimension evident is a little like Carroll's Snark hunt. Perhaps the dimension is the hunt itself, and the sense is the Snark'

---

8   In an article in which he likens translation to a metaphorical process, Gregory Rabassa claims that 'the matter of choice in translation always leaves the door open to that other possibility. We cannot be sure of ourselves. Translation is a disturbing craft because there is precious little certainty about what we are doing' (1989, 12). In the case of Panero's per-version, the adjective 'disturbing' appears to be embedded in the text, equally affecting craftsmanship and readership.

(1990, 20). The threatening Snark, and its hunt – the hunt for meaning – is what Panero would call '*un imposible real*' (1975, 16).

The self-begotten voice that opens 'Primer espasmo' seems to preclude the possibility of an author. Perversion does make the author disappear, or, at best, lead a precarious and liminal existence as a monstrous bicephalous creature. The Spanish translation of one of Harold Bloom's most recent bestsellers, *Genius: A Mosaic of One Hundred Exemplary Creative Minds*, provides a superb example. In the translator's note, Margarita Valencia Vargas writes '*Para llevar a cabo esta traducción fue necesario ubicar los libros de donde provenían las innumerables citas que ilustran el texto, con el fin de buscar después las traducciones más idóneas al español*' (2005, 13; 'In order to carry out this translation it was necessary to locate the sources for the numerous passages and quotes in the text, so that we could find the most adecuate Spanish translations'). Therefore, according to the translator, in the chapter devoted to Carroll, Panero's per-version – which is reproduced in the volume – seems to be the most adequate translation of the opening of 'The Hunting of the Snark'. It is not known what Valencia Vargas's motivations for such a choice were – whether unawareness or sheer provocation – but the fact is that the introduction to the poem in the 'Spanish Bloom' goes as follows: '*Las obras maestras de Carroll son los libros de Alicia... y La caza del Snark, cuyos espléndidos primeros versos dicen así*' ('Carroll masterpieces are *Alice...* and *The Hunt of the Snark*, whose splendid first lines go as follows'), and then the extract of Panero's perversion quoted above is reproduced in its entirety (2005, 860–861). A reference to Panero takes the form of a modest footnote, in which, after an explanation of the portmanteau nature of the term 'Snark' and its possible interpretations, the translator adds '*versión de Leopoldo María Panero*' (Bloom 2005, 860). In the endnotes of the book Panero is further erased: he becomes an almost invisible and mere four-lettered 'trad.' (Bloom 2005, 937). In this sense, it could be said that Panero has been destroyed, silenced by Carroll. But the text that the Spanish reader of Bloom's volume confronts is purely and solely of Panero's creation. From this perspective it is the Spanish author who has colonised and corrupted Carroll. Panero, thus conceived, represents a perverted Pierre Menard who literally constructs a new Carroll with his translation. As the Snark, the author is a two-headed creature, the product of an act of reciprocal cannibalism, a liminal marriage that, yet again, declares authorship to be an impossibility.[9]

---

9 For an alternative analysis of another extreme case of per-version, see Túa Blesa's discussion of Panero's version of Robert Browning's poem 'Childe Roland to the Dark Tower Came' (1995, 83).

The analysis of Panero's adaptation of Carroll demonstrates how per-version becomes a literary force that challenges its own theoretical presuppositions. Regardless of Panero's claims about fidelity, which constitute an extremely subjective notion, his idea of per-version implies a certain dose of ingenuousness. Within a Deleuzian framework, 'efecto *estético*' may be understood in terms of *affects* and *percepts*, that is, sites for the possibility of the creation of affections and perceptions on the potential reader. *Affects* and *percepts* are imbedded in expression 'that precedes contents, either in order to prefigure the rigid forms into which they are going to flow, or in order to make them take off along a line of flight or of transformation' (Deleuze and Guattari 1986, 85). The violent deterritorialisation of expression exerted by any translation and by, even more so, Panero's practice of per-version, opens multiple lines of flight for the creation of thoroughly original and unforeseen sets of affects and percepts, that is, a whole plethora of necessarily different aesthetic effects. Following the expansion of expression, sense becomes not only reversible, but also rhizomatic and multiple. The cracks Panero pretends to discover and 'seal' in the originals cannot be sealed or filled (Panero 1975, 18). The 'correction' is far from finished; the 'correction' is the crack, open to new fractures for sense to leak in an endless textual proliferation. A further instance of such open proliferation in Panero's translations can be seen in his per-versions of Barrie's *Peter Pan*.

... and Peter Pan

La caza del Snark has been previously introduced as the last of Panero's per-versions. Yet if we refer to the list of translations provided at the beginning of this chapter, we read that a translation of *Peter Pan* was published several years afterwards and purported to be by Panero. There is no mistake here, as *Peter Pan* was not translated by Panero. This judgment is supported by Túa Blesa's veiled suspicion in the endnotes to his introduction to the poet's *Cuentos Completos* (2007a), where he comments '*De todas estas traducciones la menos paneresca es la de Peter Pan, tanto que casi hace sospechar que no sea suya*' (Blesa 2007, 24; 'Of all of his translations, Panero's Peter Pan is the least "paneresque", and therefore we may suspect it is not his').[10] Nevertheless,

---

10 Panero himself denied his authorship of *Peter Pan* in an interview: '*No es verdad que yo hiciese esa traducción de Barrie. Yo hice el prólogo, pero lo de la traducción lo puso Huerga & Furcia* [sic] *para ganar más dinero*' (2006; It's not true that I did that Barry translation. I wrote the prologue, but Huerga & Furcia [*sic*] put that I did the translation so that they

regardless of who actually translated Barrie's masterful novel, the fact is that a brief analysis of the Spanish text contradicts both Panero's theories and practices of translation, and the naturally increasing progression of per-version in his earlier production. *Peter Pan* is an orthodox and classically 'faithful' translation, which, despite some 'necessary' interpretation, aims at the impossibility of the sheer linguistic conversion between two languages. Despite the normal and limited proliferation of sense brought about by almost mere linguistic transposition – which constitutes an obviously unavoidable chasm – the Spanish *Peter Pan* boasts a manifest refusal to (re)create. No expansions and no textual proliferations are generated, no evidence exists of a perverted process of translation. 'Panero's' *Peter Pan* is a silent text that does not even mark the cracks where silence may reside in the original; it is a dead translation. Its perception of the source is that of a fixed text with a fixed reading, a readerly text in Barthesian terms.[11] As such, the translation pledges loyalty to the source, a loyalty only attained by limiting and hiding its own existence, its own life as an independent text. Therefore, considering Blesa's affirmation that *'Panero es radicalmente consecuente en su práctica con sus teorías de la traducción'* (1995, 83; 'There's a radical consistency between Panero's theory and practice of translation'), it should be admitted that *Peter Pan* does not form a part of Panero's writings.

Peter Pan, however, seems to lure the crocodile of Panero's per-version throughout the poet's oeuvre. Panero's work has indeed been revisited once and again by the boy who refuses to grow up.[12] Of his numerous

---

would earn more money'). Linguistic and textual aspects of *Peter Pan* also corroborate the poet's words. For instance, the nomenclature used in the supposed translation (names of the Darlings, names of the pirates, some the boys, certain places as Neverland, etc) does not coincide with the names Panero uses throughout his oeuvre (for example, whereas the translation renders the Darlings as 'Señor y Señora Gentil', Panero always keeps the originals). It could be added that Panero's prologue to the Spanish adaptation of *Peter Pan* does not discuss translation theoretically, as the poet does in all his other translations. Panero also confirmed his lack of involvement in the translation to the author of this article in an informal meeting that took place in Las Palmas de Gran Canaria in March 2008.

11 In *S/Z*, Barthes opposed the readerly text – that is, the 'traditional' text open to the delicate, though necessarily simple and canonical, reading that plays in the interface of denotation and connotation – to the writerly text, which 'is a perpetual present, upon which no *consequent* language (which would inevitably make it past) can be superimposed' (1992, 5).

12 The following list is intended as an illustration of Barrie's *Peter Pan* presence in Panero, but does not claim to be exhaustive. The 'Poetica' that opened Panero's first publication *strictu sensu*, in *Nueve novísimos poetas españoles*, consisted of a spurious monologue by Captain Hook. Explicit references to Peter Pan are made in the titles of such poems as 'Llueve, llueve sobre el País del Nunca Jamás' (2001a, 56), 'Unas palabras para Peter Pan'

appearances, 'Hortus conclusus (Propuesta para un guión de cine)' included as an appendix to *Peter Pan* and regarded as Panero's 'original' may actually be regarded as a quintessential and *real* perversion of Barrie by Panero, inasmuch as it 'corrects', unfolds and discovers 'cracks' in the source, following the mechanisms of per-version.[13] 'Hortus conclusus' is structured like a short film script. Panero the 'translator' chooses to return, as far as genre similitude is concerned, to the original *Peter Pan, or The Boy Who Wouldn't Grow Up*, Barrie's play first staged and performed in 1904. The basic text, however, is '*basado en* Peter Pan' (Barrie 1998, 273; 'based on *Peter Pan*') and is intersected by both Walt Disney's reading of *Peter Pan* – mainly in the characterisation of Peter – and, most importantly, by Vernon Lee's supernatural tale 'A Wicked Voice'.[14] Panero's script corrupts the original *Peter and Wendy* by erasing parts of the text regarded as superfluous by the translator-interpreter, and locating the cracks in the text in order to amplify, expand and unfold motivated or unmotivated 'latent' senses. Thus the amplification of the family scenes in the first pages, or the episode of Peter and his shadow (1998, 275), may be regarded as pure per-version. A further clear example 'explains' the latent sense of the original in the scene in which Wendy is attacked by the arrows of the Lost Boys upon her arrival in Neverland. This time, however, she does not carry Peter's 'kiss' to save her: in the per-version we see Wendy '*tendida en el suelo, y en [su estómago] hay una flecha clavada en torno a la cual la sangre fluye como un río, exageradamente*' (Barrie 1998, 276; 'lying on the ground, an arrow piercing

---

(2001a, 61), 'Peter Punk' (2001a, 388) and 'Captain Hook' (2001a, 451). Apart from these titles, Panero's poetry is rich in explicit references to Barrie's novel, for instance in *Poesía Completa* (pages 38, 39, 57, 103, 110, 64, 85, 219, 490, 496 and 508 among others), *Teoría del miedo* (2001c, 67), *Erección del labio sobre la página* (2004, 109), *Los señores del alma* (2002, 113–115) and *Papá, dame la mano que tengo miedo* (2007b, 51). Barrie's characters' influence is such that it even expands to books co-written by Panero such as *¿Quién soy yo?* (with José Águedo Olivares, 2002, 28) and *Los héroes inútiles* (with Diego Medrano, 2005, 142, 157, 208, 212), for example. Some of the poet's essays are also affected by the presence of Pan, like 'Peter Pan, el asesino'. Furthermore, in *Los señores del alma* we read '*Toda mi vida me habían obsesionado los niños. Leí obsesivamente las páginas de* Peter Pan' (2002, 113; 'All my life I've been obsessed with children. I obsessively read the pages of *Peter Pan*'). The obsession with Pan in Leopoldo is such that it has ended up affecting one of its subsidiaries, Panero, the 'real' man himself. For example, in the film *Después de tantos años*, the poet's awakening in his bed is watched over by a little figurine of Tinker Bell that sits on his bedside table.

13 Túa Blesa comments how some of Panero's first writings could be read as '*los capítulos perdidos de...* Peter Pan' (2004, 14; 'the lost chapters of... *Peter Pan*').

14 A perversion of Vernon Lee's story by Panero entitled 'La voz maldita' was included in *Visión de la literatura de terror anglo-americana*. The title of Lee's book, *Hortus Vitae: Essays on the Gardening of Life* (1904), might also have inspired Panero's 'Hortus conclusus'.

[her stomach], blood flowing from the wound like a river, in an exaggerated manner').[15] Vernon Lee's palimpsestic trace is introduced as an explanation as well. Mr Darling is characterised as Magnus, the protagonist of 'A Wicked Voice', a musician who experiences an ambivalent attraction to, and fear of, the spectre of Zaffirino, the dead castrato singer who haunts him and 'perverts' his music. This intertext is deployed in order to account for Mr Darling's insanity – which is only suggested in Barrie's novel. His madness has been caused by the horrifying and haunting music of Peter Pan become Zaffirino (1998, 288–289). The effects of Lee's intertext in Panero's 'per-version' also underlie a further essential aspect only subtly suggested in Barrie's original. By making Pan into Zaffirino, a musician with the ability to produce captivatingly perilous music, the per-version links both itself and the original to Pan's mythological origins. Barrie's Peter suggests such origins: not only is he partially characterised as the Dionysian faun, hence the pipes, but he is also the reckless and unaware giver of life: Neverland comes to life only with his arrival. The violent, negative aspects of the mythological Pan, however, are played down by Barrie. Death and murder are mere childish games devised for the entertainment of the always triumphant Lost Boys. Panero 'corrects' this imbalance by making his frightening 'perversion' lean to the opposite side. Therefore Panero's 'perversion' of Barrie creates the exact effects that he claimed for his translation of Carroll. When explaining his translating procedure, the poet writes: '*he suprimido a la odiosa felicidad, ya que el humor no es feliz, pero tampoco… trágico*' (Panero 1975, 73; 'I have omitted odious happiness, since humour is not happy, nor… tragic'). As Panero states in his prologue to *Peter Pan*, '*El sueño de Peter Pan no es dulce y la literatura de L. Carroll da miedo*' (Panero 1998, 12; 'Peter Pan's dream is not sweet, and L. Carroll's literature is frightening'). Perhaps, as we read 'Hortus conclusus' we understand that Panero may indeed have attempted a further translation, the original title of which, 'perverted' by the translator, may have been *Peter Pan*.

The perversity involved in every relational reading generated by the hypertextual practice to which Genette refers (1997, 399) should be understood literally in Panero's case. The proliferating text, freed from the chains of meaning and *auctoritas*, leaks and escapes, destroys and creates in

---

15 Many other expansions of latent contents in *Peter Pan* can be found in 'Hortus conclusus', such as the characterisation of the Lost Boys as demented beasts (Barrie 1998, 276–277), the suggestion of the homoerotic attraction between Hook and Peter (Barrie 1998, 282) and the crucifixion of the sirens (Barrie 1998, 259).

an endless Dionysian whirl, always threatened by the crack which could, eventually, swallow the possibility of the literary, or, perchance, explode into the infinite. In Panero's – perhaps Barrie's – words '*Todos tememos la llegada de Peter Pan en nuestras habitaciones cerradas, de aquel que echa a volar, demonio travieso, los papeles para recogerlos después formando una nueva y sorprendente figura*' (Barrie 1998, 14; 'We all fear Peter Pan's arrival at our enclosed rooms. He blows our pages away, like a naughty demon, and then picks them up to create a new and surprising figure'). Panero's translations become yet another vehicle for the unbridled proliferation of the literary in his oeuvre. Like the arrival of Pan, his writing is whimsical, recurrent, energetic and violent in a way almost unprecedented in Spanish literature. Like life itself, it comprises Eros, the creator, and Thanatos, the destroyer. It is in this way that Panero's translations, as his poetry, become a risky enterprise: they risk total loss – the supreme loss of sense. As Derrida claims, 'a poem always runs the risk of being meaningless, and would be nothing without this risk' (2001, 90). It is that risk, however, that makes Panero's perverted re-creations teem with the powers of newborn, perhaps monstrous, creatures. These creatures, in turn, testify to the quintessential qualities of literature, if understood as a worthy, genuine and revolutionary enterprise.

References

Barrie, James M. 1998. *Peter Pan*. Trans. Panero, Leopoldo María. Madrid: Libertarias/Prodhufi.

Barthes, Roland. 1992. *S/Z*. Trans. Miller, Richard. Oxford: Blackwell.

Bassnett, Susan. 1991. *Translation Studies*. London: Routledge.

Benito Fernández, José. 1999. *El contorno del abismo. Vida y leyenda de Leopoldo María Panero*. Barcelona: Tusquets.

Benjamin, Walter. 1969. 'The task of the translator'. In *Illuminations*, edited by Arendt, Hannah. New York: Schocken Books: 69–82.

Blesa, Túa. 1995. *Leopoldo María Panero, el último poeta*. Madrid: Valdemar.

Blesa, Túa. 2004. 'La destruction fut ma Béatrice'. In *Leopoldo María Panero. Poesía completa 1970–2000*. Madrid: Visor: 7–16.

Blesa, Túa. 2007. 'Relatos de muertos'. In *Leopoldo María Panero. Cuentos completos*, 9–25. Madrid: Páginas de Espuma.

Bloom, Harold. 2005. *Genios: un mosaico de cien mentes creativas y ejemplares*. Trans. Valencia Vargas, Margarita. Bogotá: Editorial Norma.

Carroll, Lewis. 1975. *Matemática demente*. Trans. Panero, L. M. Barcelona: Tusquets.

Carroll, Lewis. 1982. *La caza del Snark: paroxismo en ocho espasmos*. Trans. Panero, L. M. Madrid: Libertarias.

Carroll, Lewis. 1998. *Complete Illustrated Lewis Carroll*. Hertfordshire: Wordsworth Editions.

Deleuze, Gilles. 1990. *The Logic of Sense*. Trans. Boundas, Constantin V. London: The Athlone Press.

Deleuze, Gilles; Guattari, Félix. 1986. *Kafka: Toward a Minor Literature*. Trans. Polan, Dana. Minneapolis: University of Minnesota.

Derrida, Jacques. 1999. 'Living on border lines'. In *Deconstruction and Criticism*. New York: Continuum:75–176.

Derrida, Jacques. 2001. *Writing and Difference*. Trans. Bass, Alan. London: Routledge.

Ducasse, Isidore (Comte de Lautréamont). 1992. *Les chants de Maldoror, poésies, lettres*. Edited by Besnier, Patrick. Paris: Le Livre de Poche.

Genette, Gérard. 1997. *Palimpsests: Literature in the Second Degree*. Trans. Newman, Channa; Doubinsky, Claude. Lincoln: University of Nebraska Press.

Isnardi, Graciela. 1979. 'El hacedor de milagros: Octavio Paz, maestro de traductores.' *Cuadernos hispanoamericanos* 343–345:720–731.

Jakobson, Roman. 2006. 'On linguistic aspects of translation'. In *Translation: Theory and Practice: A Historical Reader*, edited by Eysteinsson, Astradur; Weissbort, Daniel. Oxford: Oxford University Press.

Lear, Edward. 1972. *El ómnibus sin sentido*. Trans. Panero L. M. Madrid: Visor.

Lee, Vernon. 2006. 'A wicked voice'. In *Hauntings and Other Fantastic Tales*, edited by Maxwell, Catherine; Pulham, Patricia. Peterborough, Ontario: Broadview Press: 154–181.

López Castellano, Ramón. 2010. 'The writing of Leopoldo María Panero: Subjectivity and multiplicity'. Ph.D. thesis, Melbourne: Monash University.

Medina Domínguez, Alberto. 2001. *Exorcismos de la memoria: políticas y poéticas de la melancolía en la España de la transición*. Madrid: Ediciones Libertarias.

Panero, Leopoldo María. 1971. 'Leopoldo María Panero o el mundo del silencio'. In *Infame Turba*, edited by Federico Campbell. Barcelona: Lumen.

Panero, Leopoldo María. 1977. *Visión de la literatura de terror anglo-americana*. Madrid: Felmar.

Panero, Leopoldo María. 1984. *Dos relatos y una perversión*. Madrid: Libertarias.

Panero, Leopoldo María. 1998. *Mi cerebro es una rosa*. Ed. Benito Fernández, J. Donostia: Roger Editor.

Panero, Leopoldo María. 2001a. *Poesía completa 1970–2000*. Ed. Blesa, Túa. Madrid: Visor.

Panero, Leopoldo María. 2001b. 'Poesía y delirio'. Interviewed by Rodríguez Marcos, Javier. *El País, Babelia* 30 October. Accessed 4 May 2012. Available from: http://elpais.com/diario/2001/10/27/babelia/1004139550_850215.html.

Panero, Leopoldo María. 2001c. *Teoría del miedo*. Tarragona: Igitur.

Panero, Leopoldo María. 2002. *Los señores del alma*. (Poemas del manicomio del Dr. Rafael Inglot). Madrid: Valdemar.

Panero, Leopoldo María. 2004. *Erección del labio sobre la página*. Madrid: Valdemar.

Panero, Leopoldo María. 2006. '"A mí lo que me gustan son las poesías, no los poetas". Entrevista a Leopoldo María Panero'. Interviewed by Ruano, Joaquín. *El coloquio de los perros* 11(invierno). Accessed 4 May 2012. Available from http://www.elcoloquiodelosperros.net/numero11/olfateando.htm#leopoldo.

Panero, Leopoldo María. 2007a. *Cuentos completos*. Ed. Blesa, Túa. Madrid: Páginas de Espuma.

Panero, Leopoldo María. 2007b. *Papá, dame la mano que tengo miedo*. Barcelona: Cahoba.

Panero, Leopoldo María and Medrano, Diego. 2005. *Los héroes inútiles*. Castellón: Ellago Ediciones.

Panero, Leopoldo María and Olivares, José Águedo. 2002. *¿Quién soy yo?* Valencia: Pretextos.

Paz, Octavio. 1973. *El signo y el garabato*. México D. F.: Editorial Joaquín Mortiz.

Paz, Octavio. 1974. *Versiones y diversiones*. México D. F.: Editorial Joaquín Mortiz.

Paz, Octavio. 1979. *Poemas (1935–1975)*. Barcelona: Seix Barral.

Paz, Octavio. 1981. *Traducción: literatura y literalidad*. Barcelona: Tusquets.

Paz, Octavio. 1985. 'Octavio Paz, interview'. In *The Poet's Other Voice: Conversations on Literary Translation*, edited by Honig, Edwin. Amherst: University of Massachusetts Press.

Rabassa, Gregory. 1989. 'No two snowflakes are alike: Translation as metaphor'. In *The Craft of Translation*, edited by Biguenet, John; Schulte, Rainer. Chicago: University of Chicago Press.

Chapter 3

Parallel creations

Between self-translation and the translation of the self

Rita Wilson

In recent years, influenced to some degree by postcolonial studies, research on constructions of cultural identity has focused on aspects of 'language plurality' in literary texts. Yet, while many theorists in postcolonial literary and cultural studies have addressed the concepts of translated identities and cultures,[1] the question of what it means to migrate into another tongue has yet to be carefully examined from a translation-studies perspective. Sherry Simon theorises that, since we 'increasingly understand cultural interaction not merely as a form of exchange but as production', translation is not 'simply a mode of linguistic transfer but a translingual practice, a writing across languages which permits new kinds of conversations and new speaking positions' (Simon and St. Pierre 2000, 28). The writers located in these new speaking positions are often 'language migrants'[2] who draw on linguistic processes such as abrogation – that is, the refusal of a standard of normative or 'correct' language usage imposed by an imperial culture –

---

1   To mention just a few notable examples, Françoise Lionnet (1995) has shown that postcolonial identities are necessarily *métissées* in order to braid the multiple aspects that constitute them. *Métissage*, as a multi-voiced practice, enables writers to privilege the differences that living in multiple languages afford them and to shape hybrid identities. Niranjana Tejaswini has labelled postcolonial people as 'people living in translation' (1994, 36). Gayatri Chakravorty Spivak has established the impossibility for the translator to 'translate from a position of monolinguist superiority' (2000, 410). This impossibility demonstrates the necessity for linguistic diversity and flexibility in order to engage in 'the most intimate act of reading' that translation constitutes (409).

2   'Language migrants' is the expression that Mary Besemeres (2002) uses to describe writers who articulate their autobiographical narratives in languages that are not their mother tongues.

as well as hybridisation and creolisation to meet the challenges that they encounter when trying to translate themselves into a new linguistic code. Such a challenge, Simon suggests, proposes translation as 'a necessary means through which knowledge is tested, recontextualized, submitted to critical scrutiny' (Simon and St. Pierre 2000, 27).

To put it in slightly different terms, translingual writings[3] explicitly establish a dialogic process between the culture of origin and the host culture by addressing various frames of reference (religion, food, landscape, traditions, etc) and by highlighting common and differing aspects in the two cultures. In this way, readers are not only made familiar with cultures often remote to them, but they are also offered a view from the outside of their own culture and society, so that they can look at it from a different – and critical – angle. At the same time, while on the one hand a comparison is established, on the other hand a syncretic process is enacted, both in the gradual adjustment of the migrant protagonists to their new home and in the impact they make on the host culture and language. Armando Gnisci[4] observes that translingual writers have already undertaken 'the triple jump', going beyond multi- and interculturalism and providing a new model of 'transcultural' communication by asserting the 'dignity of outsider status' (2007). These writers celebrate migrant or diasporic cultures through what Shailja Patel calls 'migritude',[5] a term that captures the unique political and cultural space occupied by migrants who refuse to choose between identities of origin and identities of assimilation; they channel difference as a source of power rather than conceal or erase it. Works such as these that test the

---

3 Increased migration and the consequent increase in horizontal language acquisition gave rise to a new polyphonic linguistic and literary reality in the twentieth century, and there now exists a significant body of narrative texts that is variously referred to as multi-, hetero-, poly- or translingual. See, for example, Kellman (2003), Meylaerts (2006), Hokenson and Munson (2007).

4 Armando Gnisci, retired professor of Comparative Literature at La Sapienza University in Rome, was the first scholar to take an interest in so-called immigrant literature in Italy. In 1997 he created BASILI, a database on immigrant authors who write in Italian. In 2001 he launched the online journal *Kumà. Creolizzare l'Europa* http://www.disp.let. uniroma1.it/kuma/presentazione.html.

5 A neologism that is a play on 'Negritude and Migrant Attitude'. 'The four works that make up the Migritude Cycle draw on my spiritual and cultural heritage, as a 3rd-generation East African of Indian Gujurati descent. Conceived as an Epic Journey In Four Movements, Migritude references the earliest religious teaching imparted to Hindu children: that of the First Four Gods. The Hindu child is taught that her first god is her Mother. The second god is her Father. The third god is her Teacher. The fourth god is The Guest. Part I of the Migritude Cycle, When Saris Speak (The Mother), is a 90-minute spoken word theatre show. And now, a bilingual (Italian–English) book.' (Patel, 2008)

boundaries of form are essential to literary culture because they explore the limits of expression and thus the boundaries of the self.

A pivotal concept for translingual writers, who fashion narratives that try to encompass both the 'original' and the re-located cultural-linguistic self, is that of 'self-translation'.[6] Such writers, working in their adopted language, must narratively 'translate' the self that took shape in the native language in order to render it intelligible to an adoptive-language readership. Unlike the vast majority of professional translators who translate from a foreign language into their mother tongue, and whose task is to make the unfamiliar (the 'other') accessible to their home audience by presenting it in familiar linguistic forms, the language migrant performs a converse task. If we consider the narrative that articulates the pre-migration self a source text, and the narrated self that emerges from the translating act carried out for their adoptive-language audience the target text, language migrants are translating from the mother tongue to the foreign language. They are translating the self into the other.

The feminine touch

What is striking in the current literary production by language migrants in Italy is the massive presence of female writers. The reasons for this are manifold, and though their voices vary greatly since they come from different geographic, economic and political origins, they all have a propensity to represent an 'otherness' within the ambiguity and ambivalence of a bilingual and bicultural reality.[7] Some consider their bicultural situation a contradiction, while others take advantage of it in order to 'bilanguage'[8] reality and so destabilise a monolingual vision of Italy and highlight the incommensurability of the different cultures as a political commentary.

---

6   Gideon Toury identifies self-translation as autotranslation and defines it as 'translating what one has just said in one language into another; (i) to oneself (intrapersonal autotranslation) and (or: and then) (ii) to others (interpersonal autotranslation)' (1995, 244). Here, I use the term to refer both to the process of translating oneself or one's own culture in writing, as well as to a self-reflexive and inter-lingual creative process. For more on this see Wilson (2009).

7   For a recent detailed discussion of the presence of migrant women writers in the Italian literary landscape, see Contarini (2010).

8   Walter Mignolo theorises that bilanguaging 'as a condition of border thinking from the colonial difference, opens up to a postnational thinking' (2000, 254).

While the creativity and self-determination involved in writing in Italian have, in the last few decades, inspired many authors, the act of self-translation is usually accompanied by a deeply felt sense of loss of the mother tongue. As Christiana De Caldas Brito eloquently argues, the mother tongue denotes the mental make-up of the individual, and abandoning the language of childhood to replace it with a language learned as an adult is to produce a change in the quality of communication. Looking back over her own literary productions, she identifies seven phases in the 'linguistic journey of the migrant' (De Caldas Brito 2005, 35) that progress from feeling 'enclosed' in the mother tongue, to a sense of wonder at the sounds of the new language, to a stage when the two languages intermingle and, finally, to a recognition of the need for new words, followed by, in her case, a decision to choose Italian as the language of communication. This choice enables De Caldas Brito to become socially and politically active in her new country and, ultimately, to be sufficiently in command of the language to use it creatively and even playfully (De Caldas Brito 2005, 35, 37, 39, 41, 43, 44).

In what follows, I examine the processes of self-translation in the linguistic journeys of four women writers, for whom writing in an additional language is like flipping out another 'badge of identity' (Buruma 2003, 19): Ribka Sibhatu, Geneviève Makaping, Ubax Cristina Ali Farah and Maria Abbebù Viarengo. Their pioneering works arise from the double need to give voice to the experience of immigrants and to familiarise Italians with the cultures of origin of their new neighbours, fulfilling, therefore, a function of cultural mediation. Translation, in a broad sense, is presented as a necessary condition of writing and, subsequently, reading. In their narratives, self-translation, mistranslation, back translation and/or zero translation are used in order to liberate and express a translingual imagination.

Double inscription of her self: Ribka Sibhatu

There are many acts of translation in the life of Eritrean-born Ribka Sibhatu, beginning when she disguises herself as a country woman (braiding her hair to pass as someone from a lower class) and smuggles herself across the border into Ethiopia. Hers is a journey in translation: from her native Tigrinya into the language of her primary education – Amharic – in Addis Abeba; to French when she fled to France after her marriage; and finally to Italian when she moved to Rome, where she earned a degree in Modern Languages and Literatures from La Sapienza University. The material experience of travelling is directly related to Sibhatu's acquisition of cultural, and linguistic, dynamism.

Translation of identity through disguise, migration and language is at the core of her innovative first book, *Aulò: Canto-poesia dall'Eritrea* (1993), a narrative written in Italian with a parallel text in Tigrinya.[9] The Italian text is presented on the left side of the book – thus investing it with the authority of normative reading – while the ethio-semitic characters used in the Tigrinya writing system on the right acquire an ancillary, decorative, 'othering' function for the European reader. This bilingual text is both exemplary of the notion of self-translation as a double writing process, in which each text produced is a variant of the other, and of the view that the act of self-translation represents a 'literary encounter which opens autobiographical spaces' (Nikolau 2006, 27). Sibhatu's is a game of appropriation and accountability in which she shifts between her 'original' self and her translated self, and in which she practises a politics of resistance whereby the act of linguistic translation is not fully accomplished but undermined by the parallel text in Tigrinya. While the traces of difference are visibly present, the facing texts also reveal a dialogism, a continuity between original and translation that conveys Bakhtin's concept of heteroglossia in a concrete way: both the typography and the illustrations that accompany the text accentuate the multiplicity of languages and heritages embedded in the narrative discourse. There is an implicit belief in the faithfulness of the translator so that the reader may have a sense of parallel motions of meaning and images on both sides of the book.

Sibhatu's bilingual text is a clear case of self-translation, but it is also one that presents a form of deviance from the commonly understood practice of self-translation, in that it requires several processes of mediation. She is not, in fact, the idiomatic bilingual described by Hokenson and Munson, someone equally able to write in both languages and to reproduce standard and normative discourse of sufficient quality as to retain the author's original meaning in both texts without the interference of an editor (Sibhatu 1998, 13–14). First, she requires the mediation of a fellow Eritrean, to render her 'Roman Tigrinya' into 'Tuscan Tigrinya' (6). Second, the act of translating the self from the 'mother tongue' into the familiar but not perfectly commanded Italian language requires a further process of mediation by the editor. Sibhatu does not, therefore, produce the 'authentic' translation aspired to by Spivak (2000). She does, however, use both languages to simultaneously mark and

---

9 Tigrinya is spoken in the Eritrean highlands, in Asmara and in the Ethiopian region of Tigray. It should not be confused with Tigrè, which is only spoken in Eritrea.

erase her difference, revealing the continuity and discontinuity within both traditions. Sibhatu affirms that choosing to write in Italian was motivated by her need to communicate directly with her host society and raise awareness of the increasingly multicultural aspects of that culture.[10] At the same time, the use of Tigrinya is testimony of the continuity of her engagement with her original language and culture. This is further emphasised by the choice of the particular genre of performance poetry, the *aulò* (also known as the *massè*), a genre often performed at social gatherings or important occasions such as wedding celebrations or commemorations. The declamatory style favoured by the latter is effectively illustrated by the two *aulò* dedicated to the author's grandmother Hiriti, in recognition of her status as 'tribe elder' and her role as adviser to political and military leaders (Sibhatu 1998, 60–61).

Sibhatu attempts to live across boundaries, searching for freedom by wearing several 'language skins' (Steiner 1975, 473 and *passim*), shifting her focus from private to public, from oral to written, from local to global. On the one hand, the veil of secrecy provided by the two 'language skins' helps to maintain her individual freedom and her own territory. On the other hand, the two facing languages and cultures enter into mutual interpenetration through a process of transculturation.[11] The confrontation between languages creates mutual cultural contamination and establishes a process of transformation – for both the Italian and the Tigrinya reader.

The view from across the other side: Geneviève Makaping

While Ribka Sibhatu opts to make the process of self-translation visible through the dual-language presentation of her text, Geneviève Makaping chooses to foreground processes of self-translation as acts of symbolic self-assertion and empowerment in her first book *Traiettorie di sguardi. E se gli altri foste voi?* ('The trajectory of the gaze. What if *they* were you?', 2001).

---

10 '*[I testi] Li ho concepiti e scritti mentre già vivevo qui , mi sentivo di casa e mi sembrava naturale scrivere qualcosa che il pubblico italiano potesse comprendere, C'era quindi anche una volontà comunicativa.*' Interview with Daniele Comberiati, quoted at http://www.360gradisud.it/index.php?option=com_content&view=article&id=215:scritture-migrate&catid=18:parlano-di-noi&Itemid=4.

11 The term was first used by ethnographers to describe how marginal groups select and invent from material transmitted to them by the dominant cultures. Mary Louise Pratt defines transculturation as a phenomenon of the contact zone: 'social spaces where disparate cultures meet, clash and grapple with each other, often in highly asymmetrical relations of dominance and subordination' (1992, 4).

A naturalised Italian from Cameroon and an anthropologist by training, she uses the methodology of participant observation in which the gaze is reversed so that the narration of her personal experience as an object of violence and intolerance becomes a study of 'native' Italians: *'Guardo me che guarda loro che da sempre mi guardano'* (2001, 40; 'I look at myself looking at those who have always looked at me', italics in original).[12]

Makaping operates a deconstruction of the 'ideology of exclusion' (2001, 55), which she identifies as the dominant marker of European identity, by defining her speaking position as one that is 'eccentric' (in the sense of both 'ex-centric' and 'unconventional'):

> *Appartengo ad un centro che non è di* loro. *E loro mi trovano bizzarra. Mi sento anche privilegiata, rispetto a quelli* come me, *dal momento che io posso parlare,* non accettare, dire di no, non annuire; *io sono il centro di quelli* come me, *e tutti insieme poi siamo il margine. Sono una sineddoche, la parte per il tutto, il singolare per il plurale.* (2001, 137)

> I belong to a centre that does not belong to *them*. And they find me weird. I also feel privileged, compared to those *like me*, since I can talk, *refuse, say no, disagree,* I am the centre of those *like me*, and all of us together are the margin. I am a synecdoche, the part for the whole, the singular for the plural.

The emphasis on *'quelli* come me' (those *like me*) evokes that concept of mimicry which Homi Bhabha uses to describe the projection of the self as performed by minors. He notes that in the textuality of (post)colonialism, mimicry addresses difference – members of a colonised society who engage in mimicry are *almost the same* as the colonisers, *but not quite*. Mimicry becomes a discourse 'uttered between the lines and as such both against the rules and within them' (Bhabha 1992, 89). Mimicry appropriates and distorts the model proposed as dominant – and therefore normative – by giving back a gaze of otherness, shattering from the margins the unity of the hegemonic group. This is analogous to Makaping's strategy of creating a new linguistic code by deconstructing and reconstructing given meanings and concepts in the dominant (Italian) discourse, beginning with asserting the right both to name herself (*'Voglio essere io a dire come mi chiamo'* 2001, 31) and to classify herself as black (*'chiamatemi negra'* 2001, 36).

---

12 All translations from Italian are mine unless otherwise indicated.

The border is often the place where the first act of self-translation takes place, as one of the very first things to be translated is the language migrant's name. The translation can be literal: an Italian equivalent of the language migrant's original name is chosen to represent her in the new country;[13] or phonetic: the language migrant's original name is 'translated' by 'Italianising' its pronunciation.[14] The practice of Italianisation of names is not innocuous. It is an attempt to normalise whatever seems deviant or different and has the effect of appropriating identity. Makaping resists this misappropriation of identity and experience. Her self-translation is an attempt to create a space in which the previously marginalised can affirm their own subjectivity and can articulate their own perception of the world:

> *Se sai scrivere il tuo nome e pronunciarlo, potresti rivolgerti al tuo denominatore nella sua stessa lingua. Se sai il tuo nome, per forza saprai anche il suo* (2001, 55).
>
> If you know how to write and pronounce your name, you would be able to speak to those who name you in their own language. If you know your name, of course you will also know theirs.

In Spivak's terms, Makaping is a 'competent native informant', that is, someone who can speak for her native group to outsiders. She is acutely aware that language is not only related to power in a bigger picture in society; it is also related to power in a smaller picture, for individuals in their efforts to construct identities that allow access to resources in their host societies. Language in this sense is a kind of password. If you understand the language responsively and are able to manipulate it, you pass; if you have access to the more highly valued form of that language, you gain a more prestigious identity. In other words, to construct an identity that allows access, you need to master the language first. Makaping underlines the fact that Italian is not the only language present in these texts, and it is not taken for granted that it should be:

---

13 As in, for example, '*Mustafa diventa Mino, e Hussein diventa Enzo*' (Wakkas 1995, 143). The preservation and/or modification of names is a recurring issue in Italian migrant writing, and dates back to the 1990s with Mohamed Bouchane's *Chiamatemi Alì*.

14 '*Gli europei mi chiamano Ribka, Rebka, Rebecca. In realtà mi chiamo Rebqā*' (Sibhatu 1998, 10)'.

La mia espressione linguistica invece è ancora solo 'traduzione' in italiano di concetti pensati in chissà quante altre lingue contemporaneamente: il francese, il pidgin, l'inglese e la mia lingua madre che è il bahuanese del Camerun. (79)

My linguistic expression is still only a 'translation' into Italian of concepts simultaneously in who knows how many other languages: French, Pidgin, English and my mother tongue, which is Cameroonian Bahuanese.

It is not only a problem of code, as Makaping underlines. The interiorisation of any new language is the starting point both for recognising the plurality of the identities acquired by the author, and for questioning the completeness and integrity of her subjectivity: '*a prescindere dalla mia conoscenza delle lingue, devo comunque riconoscere di avere un'identità caleidoscopica o a mosaico*' (2001, 80; 'regardless of my knowledge of languages, I have to recognise that my identity is kaleidoscopic, a mosaic').

Makaping's provocative text illustrates the power of a 'migratory vision' derived from heterolingual techniques (Bhabha 1992, 185). Her approach is akin to that process of doubling that Bhabha describes as extracting the canonic meaning from 'narratives of originary and initial subjectivities' in order to resignify them. Innovative combinations of discourse are produced through an 'unpicking' and relinking that 'retranslate' normative discourses (1992, 185). This tendency to retranslate and relink in its use of 'non-European' elements is shared by Ubax Cristina Ali Farah, in whose heteroglossic work the friction present between different linguistic and cultural strata is made transparent.

Living and writing in translation: Ubax Cristina Ali Farah

Born in Italy, Ubax Cristina Ali Farah spent her childhood in Mogadishu, where she often acted as a translator for her mother, who never learnt Somali. Her first novel, *Madre piccola* (2007), presents a main character, Domenica Axad, who, like the author, has a Somali father and an Italian mother, and who, again like the author, programmatically signifies her dual identity in the use of both her Somali and Italian first names. After her parents' separation, Domenica Axad is caught between two different worlds and cultures. She develops self-injurious behaviour and only stops this once she is able to 'knot the threads together again', to use the metaphor that recurs throughout the whole novel; the threads are those of her own double identity as well as that of her people dispersed in the diaspora caused by the Somali civil war at the start of the 1990s.

The theme of a 'braided' identity is presented in the incipit of the novel:

> Soomaali baan ahay*[15], come la mia metà che è intera. Sono il filo sottile, così sottile che si infila e si tende, prolungandosi. Così sottile che non si spezza. E il groviglio di fili si allarga e mostra, chiari e ben stretti, i nodi, pur distanti l'uno dall'altro, che non si sciolgono. Sono una traccia in quel groviglio e il mio principio appartiene a quello multiplo. (Ali Farah 2007, 1)

> Soomaali baan ahay*, like my half that is whole, I am the fine thread, so fine that it slips through and stretches, getting longer. So fine that it does not snap. And the tangled mass of threads widens and reveals the knots, clear and tight, that, though far from each other, do not unravel. I am one thread in that tangled mass and my beginning belongs to the multiple one. (Ali Farah 2011, 1)

The opening words unequivocally affirm the narrating voice's Somali identity. At the same time, the Italian translation of the Somali phrase ('Somalo io sono'; 'I am Somali'), which is provided in a footnote, alerts the reader to the interplay of linguistic and cultural subjectivities within the novel, which is conceived as a tale told by many voices, differing from chapter to chapter. The process of self-translation is directly evidenced in the table of contents, in which the titles of the chapters indicate the move back and forth between the Italian narrating voice (Domenica) and the Somali narrating voice (Axad).

While Ali Farah's self-conscious use of language differs in several ways from Makaping's, they both share the idea that the act of speaking is also the act of being spoken; and the need to name the self to another persists. Consider, for example, the introduction of Domenica's cousin Barni (the 'little mother' of the novel's title):

---

15 It is the refrain of a poem composed by Cabdulqaadir Xirsi Siyaad, 'Yamyam' (1977). He was one of the most important poets of socialist Somalia and his writings, which were among the first to appear once Somali became a written language in 1972, were disseminated by readings on radio.

allora, cominciamo. Dal mio nome, certo. Mi chiamo Barni Sharmaarke.
Attenta, lo scriva correttamente. No, non è difficile. Deve solo scegliere quale
codice usare. Il vostro o il nostro. Sui documenti fanno tanti di quei pasticci.
Non solo per la trascrizione; il problema è soprattutto con i cognomi. A me
sembra così semplice. È che noi usiamo il patronimico al posto del cognome.
(2007, 13–14).

Good, let's start. With my name, sure. My name is Barni Sharmaarke.
Careful, spell it correctly. No, it's not difficult. You just have to pick a
linguistic code. Yours or ours. They always make such a big mess on
official documents. They don't just have problems with the transcription;
the big problem is with last names. It seems so simple to me. You see,
we use the patronymic instead of the last name. (2011, 12–13)

The choice to speak (and to write) in Italian is not conscious when it is forced
by the necessity of migration, but becomes conscious when it is perceived
as part of one's identity, *'come la mia metà che è intera'* ('like my half that is
my whole'), as Ali Farah writes in the first line of *Madre piccola*. The whole
novel can be seen as a 'translation' from orality to the written text, as the plot
is completed when Domenica Axad finally writes down the oral tales she
has collected, mirroring Ali Farah's own writing practice (Comberiati 2007,
46). In the process of self-translating from oral Somali to written Italian,
Ali Farah practises 'code-mixing' in the sense used by eminent linguist,
Braj B. Kachru; that is, 'the use of lexical items or phrases from one code
in the stream of discourse of another' (2006, 273). At the heart of such
code-mixing is the strategy he defines as *neutralisation*: 'used to "unload" a
linguistic item from its traditional, cultural and emotional connotations by
avoiding its use and choosing an item from another code. The borrowed item
has referential meaning, but no cultural connotations in the context of the
specific culture' (2006, 273).

Translingual writers have recourse to their own mother tongues, inserting
them into their adopted language (in this case Italian), thus rendering the
latter the base on which other languages are grafted, creating new and
original solutions. Code-mixing modulates intercultural encounters in
which the language is contaminated and distorted. As Ali Farah says in an
interview, she wants to invert the power relationship between the languages
by inscribing one within the other and thus making an effort to initiate a
process of renewal (*'svecchiamento'*) of the Italian language (quoted in Nur
Goni 2005–2006, 45–47).

In *Madre piccola*, heteroglossia has a narratological function. The Somali words and expressions are an integral part of the discourse, sometimes accompanied by an Italian equivalent, sometimes left untranslated. As the narrative progresses, these words become familiar to the reader and do not constitute a language or knowledge barrier – rather they convey a concept that would not be conveyed with equal impact in Italian. Through self-translation Ali Farah also introduces the principle of plurality into the unity of the writing subject, thus decentring the position of the author. Writing through translation is a strategy that aims at accumulating as many points of view as possible. Each time a text gets translated into another language a new standpoint is reached, allowing the original thought to be viewed from a completely different angle. The author, through the voice of the protagonist, develops a series of metalinguistic reflections that are germane to the other texts under consideration here. The message that is conveyed – that is, not taking a language for granted – is a fundamentally important one, especially for monolingual (mother-tongue) readers who do not, generally, reflect on a tool that they have had since birth. Those who have never been immersed in a foreign language can easily take their own language for granted, while that language is seen from quite a different perspective by someone who lives in two distinct language worlds. There are numerous references to such a double register in *Madre piccola*, specifically to draw attention to the fact that being bilingual is both a privilege and a responsibility, especially when that bilingual is also an author-translator-mediator:

> *Vivevo la traduzione come un divertimento, a tratti, ma più spesso con un forte senso di responsabilità, soprattutto quando si trattava di limare le asprezze, di non lasciar trapelare sentimenti negativi. Ero alle prese con voci schiette che scaturivano dall'animo prive di filtri. Voci consegnate a me traghettatrice senza che l'emittente si sforzasse di adattarle al destinatario. Divenni una grande conoscitrice dell'animo umano, in virtù di questo esercizio quotidiano con il quale mi allenavo a capire gli adulti nei loro recessi più profondi.* (2007, 232–233)

> I lived translation as an entertainment sometimes, but more often with a strong sense of responsibility, especially when I had to tone down harshness, to hide negative feelings. I was dealing with blunt utterances that sprung unfiltered from the soul. Voices that were entrusted to me to ferry across without the speaker making any effort to adapt them to the receiver. I acquired a profound knowledge of the human soul, thanks to this daily exercise that trained me to understand the deepest recesses of the adult mind. (2011, 202)

Domenica Axad epitomises the translator who mediates not only between languages and cultures but is also the locus (or meeting place) of internalised dispositions and societal norms. Ali Farah, like Sibhatu and Makaping, is intensely aware of her role as mediator – a role that is charged with immense responsibility – and as someone who occupies the liminal space in between cultures. Operating from a position of plurality, she uses her authorial position to move the emphasis from sociocultural relevance to representationality. It is precisely the need to represent herself – to establish her own authority and identity – rather than a desire for verisimilitude, that determines the use of 'other' languages in Maria Abbebù Viarengo's writing.

Writing the self into public existence: Maria Abbebù Viarengo

One of the most experimental writers within this group of language migrants, Maria Abbebù Viarengo creates a discourse on *métissage*[16] and multiple identities, which brings together the personal and the theoretical, autobiographical narrative and public discussions of otherness. Born of an Ethiopian mother from the Oromo language group, and of a Piedmontese father, she is another example of a biologically interracial daughter who 'braids' her languages and cultures in a transcultural move that appropriates and modifies the standardised platform of Italian literature, and creates cultural spaces in which other perspectives are represented.

---

16 *Métissage* is a site for writing and surviving in the 'interval between different cultures and languages' (Lionnet 1989, 1); a way of merging and blurring genres, texts and identities; an active literary stance, a political strategy and a pedagogical praxis. As *métis* has been re-appropriated from its original and negative meaning 'half-breed', following Lionnet we appropriate métissage from its original meaning of 'mixed-blood' to become an alternative metaphor for fluidity, and a creative strategy for the braiding of gender, race, language and place into autobiographical narratives. Literary métissage not only describes experience; it is a strategy for interpreting and critiquing the experiences reported. At the same time these autobiographical texts provide apertures for understanding and questioning the multiple conditions and contexts which give rise to those experiences; and the particular languages, memories, stories and places in which these experiences are located and created. Literary métissage offers the possibility for writing and telling stories which are rooted in history and memory, but which are also stories of becoming. These texts generate knowledge about repressed cultural and individual memories, traditions and mother tongues. Literary métissage is seen as a hopeful act initiating a 'genuine dialogue with the dominant discourse(s)' in order to transform these discourses, thus 'favoring exchange rather than provoking conflict' (Lionnet 1989, 3).

Viarengo's autobiography, *Koborò e Violini io non scelgo* ('Koborò and Violins I don't choose'), has been described as an 'ego-document' (Ponzanesi 143) which is explicitly intended as a form of dialogue with the author's mother and a recovery of a forgotten language, Oromo Imbecu (Viarengo 1990, 75). In 1990, the literary journal, *Linea d'Ombra,* published an extract from her autobiography under the title 'Andiamo a spasso?' ('Shall we go for a walk?'). The publisher's unilateral decision to translate the original Oromo title ('Scirscir 'n demna') into Italian – thus effectively erasing the mother's heritage – resulted in Viarengo's refusal to publish the text if subjected to such linguistic intervention, and the full autobiography remains unpublished to date.[17]

The overlapping of languages is an important aspect of the dichotomy that Viarengo has inscribed on her body and in her work in what is effectively both a biological and a literary *métissage* exemplified by the portrayal of the different naming practices in her two cultures: her father recalls that when she was born he told her maternal grandmother:

> I'd like to call you Maria, after my aunt. I'd named your sister after my mother. Your grandmother said I could call you what I liked, and it was right I should, but, 'You know, we don't name babies as soon as they're born. To give them a name we have to understand who they are. So we have to wait a while. Watch them,' she said. So it was that, after a while, the grandmother chose. 'This baby is Abbebec. Full of flowers. She who wants to bloom, to know.'
>
> My name is Abbebec.
>
> I was the baby of the house and my mother caressed and called me by my pet name: Abbebu. As everyone in Ghidami has always done.
>
> But now, was I Abbebu or Maria?
>
> Here in Italy I could have abandoned Abbebu and let Maria take up all the space inside me, she was, after all the one who'd been given more room to emerge. But Abbebu, whom I loved so much, clung to the walls of Maria's soul and didn't mean to disappear. (Viarengo, Scirscir 'n demna: extracts from an autobiography 2000, 21–22)[18]

---

17 Chapter 8 has been published in an English translation by Aamer Hussein in *Wasafiri* in 2000.

18 The Italian version of this excerpt remains unpublished. The English translation is the only available published version.

Writing her life in Italian becomes the thread that weaves together the fragments constituting Viarengo's *métisse* identity. By narratively weaving her different selves, she attempts to create a space in which chronological order is destroyed, and past and present can be rewritten synchronically. Self-translation is a way for Viarengo to reconcile her two languages and cultures through a process of recreation and rewriting – not only of her work but of her self and her world – that favours a double, in-between identity. Nevertheless, like De Caldas Brito, she experiences a prevalent sense of loss: there are wide gaps in her history that cannot be filled, and she writes of the difficulty of self-identifying with any one culture while others struggle to 'identify' her, calling her: *'anfez, klls, meticcia, mulatta, caffelatte, half-cast, ciuculatin, colored, armusch... indiana, araba... siciliana'* (Viarengo 1990, 74). Viarengo resists all attempts to fit her into a neat pigeon hole, recalling how she has always moved among three languages: Oromo, Italian and the local Turin dialect. The translation from one vernacular to another is a thread uniting the old life and the new. Language, which is usually talked about in terms of the dividing line between us and them, the global and the local, in her case operates as a flexible mediation: 'I have inside me fragments of many languages: Oromo, Amharic, Tigrina [*sic*], English, Arabic, of gestures, tastes, religions, perfumes, costumes, feasts, sounds, music, looks, faces, places, spaces, silences' (Viarengo 2000, 21).

Many cultures and sublanguages interfere with the dominant one. Viarengo's father's Piedmontese constituted a specification within Italian as much as her mother's Oromo was for the Amharic-speaking community. When she moves from Ghidami to Turin, it is the Piedmontese dialect that gives her a sense of belonging in Italy, not the 'national' Italian language. In her writing, Viarengo uses entire sentences in Piedmontese (without glossary or translation) which locate her in the community, bonding her with anyone capable of understanding Piedmontese, but also excluding any reader who is not located within that very specific culture. She does the same with Oromo words, which are naturally blended with the Italian language as if in some inexplicable way they are capable of recreating a duality in the sameness: *'[mamma] ci portava a scircir e ci preparava il faffatò'* (1990, 76; '[mum] would take us *scircir* and prepare the *faffatò*'). Through the insertion of the vernacular, Viarengo plays up the complexity of her translation process: the representation of non-standard speech varieties within a language invites readers to confront and interpret the diversity within that language, within that speech community – diversity of class, region, education, age. In

Viarengo's case, this is accompanied by the representation of heterophone languages, thus forcing readers to confront and interpret the multiplicity of speech communities in the world, the impossibility of understanding the speech of communities other than their own, and their own position in a polylingual context.

Viarengo constructs a translingual space – an 'extra territory' akin to Makaping's 'ex-centric' space – in which to position herself both as a Piedmontese and as an Oromo. Functioning as as a strategy of exclusion, the vernacular undermines the binary relation of the centre to the periphery, offering a continual play of resistance and creating 'tensions and contradictions within the dominant discourse, setting in motion the dynamics of dissent, intervention and change that can ultimately allow a "minority" position to resist integration ad assimilation' (Lionnet 1995, 334). Viarengo's text resists appropriation because the inclusion of Oromo and Piedmontese dialect in the Italian text creates an opacity in the text for both the non-Oromo- and the non-Piedmontese-speaker. This opacity has a double subversive function: it marks the text as radically 'other' for an Italian speaker, increasing the distance between author and reader, between insider and outsider, thus preventing any simplistic understanding based on the purely referential value of vernacular terms. Her choice to juxtapose languages in her text without mediation is directly related to how she perceives her self: 'I think, I dream, I write using the languages that I have met in my life: Italian, Piedmontese, Oromo, Arabic and English. This is what I am. In my mind I do not translate when I think a word in a language' (quoted in Luraschi 2009, 17).

In my opinion, it is the lack of translation that makes Viarengo's text highly empathetic. Lack of translation does not mean that the author does not want to communicate, or that her autobiographical narrative is solipsistic writing. Rather, her work is the concrete expression of the plurality of identities, a creative and experimental writing that gives an idea of the cohabitation of more than one identity within an individual. I think that the potentiality of untranslated expression goes beyond the juxtaposition of languages and identities. In the case of purposeful untranslatability, such as Viarengo's, the same untranslatability is meaningful. The unsaid, the not immediately understandable, the untranslated, amplify the text's meanings: these are effective ways to represent the often contradictory dimension of those who live in between two cultures. Through this literary expedient, Viarengo sets a new perspective for the writing of social relationships.

Concluding remarks

It is the comparison of divergent models of discourse that challenges the literary canon and provides a context for the development of new identity profiles, be they aesthetic, social or cultural. The translingual writer who composes in more than one language is an artist who aspires to both experience her own maternal linguistic reality and transcend it by simultaneously taking on the language of the Other. The act of multilingual creation reflects a desire to enter, know and become the Other, and then share two spheres of cultural and linguistic formation through the process of transculturation. These writers are proud of their linguistic heritage and almost invariably want to maintain their ability to write in their mother tongue: thus there is no desire for 'vertical' translation here, of giving enhanced prestige to the 'new' language, but rather of establishing a linguistic relationship of horizontality, reaching out to explore the possibilities of expression in another language of equal importance and perhaps also of understanding what it is like to achieve linguistic identification with another reality. Arguably, the multidimensionality of these translingual narratives is the consequence of an epistemological reflection about the power and the limits of the (monolingual) word. Their literary experimentation should be placed into the context of the multi-, poly-, hetero- and translingual reality that their authors inhabit. They are the 'new' nomadic citizens that Meylaerts characterises as 'polyglots travelling in between languages, in a permanent stage of (self-) translation' (Meylaerts 2006, 1). Understanding how the process of linguistic self-translation works through the textually reconstructed experiences of others allows us to define how these experiences can be translated into accessible knowledge for other nomadic citizens to use.

References

Ali Farah, Ubax Cristina. 2011. *Little Mother*. Trans. Bellesia-Contuzzi, Giovanna; Offredi Poletto, Victoria; Di Maio, D. Bloomington: Indiana University Press.

Ali Farah, Ubax Cristina. 2007. *Madre piccola*. Rome: Frassinelli.

Bakhtin, Mikhail. 1981. *The Dialogic Imagination: Four Essays*. Trans. Emerson, Caryl; Holoquist, Michael. Austin: University of Texas Press.

Besemeres, Mary. 2002. Translating One's Self: Language and Selfhood in Cross-Cultural Autobiography. Oxford: Peter Lang.

Bhabha, Homi. 1984. 'Of mimicry and man: The ambivalence of colonial discourse'. *October* 28 (Spring): 125–133.

Bhabha, Homi. 1992. *The Location of Culture*. New York: Routledge.

Bouchane, Mohamed. 1990. *Chiamatemi Alì*. Milan: Leonardo.

Buruma, Ian. 2003. 'The road to Babel'. In *Switching languages: Translingual writers reflect on their craft*, edited by Kellman, S. G. Lincoln: University of Nebraska Press: 9–24.

Comberiati, Daniele. 2007. *La quarta sponda*. Milano: Pigreco.

Contarini, Silvia. 2010. 'Narrazioni, migrazioni e genere'. In *Certi confini. Sulla letteratura italiana dell'immigrazione*, edited by Quaquarelli, Lucia. Milan: Morellini Editore: 119–159.

De Caldas Brito, Christiana. 2005. 'Il percorso linguistico dei migranti'. In *Allattati dalla lupa*, edited by Gnisci, Armando. Rome: Sinnos Editrice: 35–47.

Gnisci, Armando. 2007. 'Editoriale'. *Kumà, Creolizzare l'Europa* 13 (March). Accessed 8 July 2009. Available from http://www.disp.let.uniroma1.it/kuma/editoriale13.html.

Goni, Raimonda Nur. 2005–2006. 'Il frutto candito dell'esilio'. M.A. thesis, Venice: Università Ca' Foscari.

Hokenson, Jan Walsh; Munson, Marcella, eds. 2007. *The Bilingual Text: History and Theory of Literary Self-Translation*. Manchester: St. Jerome Publishing.

Kachru, Braj B. 2006. 'The alchemy of English'. In *The Post-Colonial Studies Reader*, edited by Bill Ashcroft et al., London and New York: Routledge: 272–275.

Kellman, Steven G, ed. 2003. *Switching Languages: Translingual Writers Reflect on Their Craft*. Lincoln: University of Nebraska Press.

Lionnet, Françoise. 1989. *Autobiographical Voices: Race, Gender, Self Portraiture*. Ithaca: Cornell University Press.

Lionnet, Françoise. 1995. *Postcolonial Representations: Women, Literature, Identity*. Ithaca: Cornell University Press.

Luraschi, Moira. 2009. 'Beyond words: Mirroring identities of Italian postcolonial women writers'. *Enquire* 3 (June): 1–22.

Makaping, Geneviève. 2001. *Traiettorie di sguardi. E se gli altri foste voi?* Catanzaro: Rubettino Editore.

Meylaerts, Reine. 2006. 'Heterolingualism in/and translation: How legitimate are the Other and his/her language? An introduction.' *Target* 18 (1): 1–15.

Mignolo, Walter. 2006. *Local Histories/Global Designs*. Princeton: Princeton University Press.

Nikolau, Paschalis. 2006. 'Notes on translating the self'. In *Translation and Creativity: Perspectives on Creative Writing and Translation Studies*, edited by Loffredo, Eugenia; Perteghella, Manuela. London: Continuum: 19–32.

Patel, Shailja. 2008. 'On migritude part I: When saris speak – The mother'. *Altre Modernità*, interview by Emanuele Monegato (July 15): 235–239. Accessed 20 September 2011. Available from http://riviste.unimi.it/index.php/AMonline/article/viewFile/300/422.

Ponzanesi, Sandra. 2004. *Paradoxes of Postcolonial Culture: Contemporary Women's Writing of the Indian and Afro-Italian Diaspora*. Albany: State University of New York Press.

Pratt, Mary Louise. 1992. *Imperial Eyes: Travel Writing and Transculturation*. London: Routledge.

Sibhatu, Ribka. 1998. *Aulò. Canto-poesia dall'eritrea*. 2nd edition. Rome: Sinnos Editrice.

Simon, Sherry; St. Pierre, Paul. 2000. *Changing the Terms: Translating in the Postcolonial Era*. Ottawa: University of Ottawa Press.

Spivak, Gayatri Chakravorty. 2000. 'The politics of translation'. In *The Translation Studies Reader*, edited by Venuti, Lawrence. New York: Routledge: 397–416.

Steiner, George. 1975. *After Babel: Aspects of Language and Translation*. Oxford: Oxford University Press.

Tejaswini, Niranjana. 1994. 'Colonialism and the politics of translation'. In *An Other Tongue: Nation and Ethnicity in the Linguistic Borderlands*, edited by Arteaga, Alfred. Durham: Duke University Press: 35–52.

Toury, Gideon. 1995. *Descriptive Translation Studies and Beyond*. Amsterdam: John Benjamins.

Viarengo, Maria Abbebù. 1990. 'Andiamo a spasso?' *Linea d'ombra* 54: 74–78.

Viarengo, Maria Abbebù. 2000. 'Scirscir 'n demna: extracts from an autobiography'. *Wasafiri* 31: 20–22.

Wakkas, Yousef. 1995. 'Io marokkino con due kappa'. In *Le voci dell'arcobaleno*, edited by Sangiorgio, R; Ramberti, A. Santarcangelo di Romagna: Fara Editore: 105–152.

Wilson, Rita. 2009. 'The writer's double: Translation, writing and autobiography'. *Romance Studies* 27 (3) (July): 186–198.

Chapter 4

Giving birth to the self

On self-translation

Ouyang Yu

If translation is the work of someone who gives birth to someone else in another language, self-translation is the work of someone who gives birth to himself in the language he was born or second-born in. Translator Xie Tianzhen once said, '原作者死亡, 译者诞生', or '*yuan zuozhe siwang, yizhe dansheng*' (Meng and Li 2005, 410; 'As the original author dies, the translator is born'). For me, the process of self-translation involves as much shame as pleasure, and acquires a kind of stain that greatly resembles that of an Australian convict. For 17 years between 1991 and 2008, none of my self-translations in English – neither poetry nor fiction – were published as such, as they were all subsumed under three words only: 'By Ouyang Yu'.

The editors were not to blame; I was. In those days, the shame was associated with a fear that I might be found lacking if I submitted work that I had translated from my own writings. At that time the word 'self-translation' was hardly ever heard and was rarely read in books of translation theory, certainly not in the histories of translation in China, where I originally come from.

The fear proved true when my attempts at submitting work acknowledged as 'Written in Chinese by Ouyang Yu and translated into English by Ouyang Yu' were met with either stony silence or immediate rejection. It led to a change of tactics on my part. To avoid perennial rejection, I covered up all the traces of self-translation by erasing that paratextual information completely.[1] When

---

1   I provide a list of poems self-translated but not acknowledged as thus, as follows: 'I have said it all wrong' and 'Life', in *Going Down Swinging*: 1995, 62–64; 'Moon', 'Night'

I compiled my own list of publications, there were categories of poetry, fiction, non-fiction and literary translation, but never of self-translation.

My fear also had something to do with being found to be unoriginal, as one constantly heard the accusation or imagined one heard it: 'If you are good enough, why not try writing in English? Why translate yourself when no great authors have ever been heard to practise such secretive acts?' The fear, ultimately, had to do with being caught lying, an imaginary finger pointed at me accusingly: 'How can you pretend that the reader is encountering your writing firsthand when it has been wrangled through a secondary, once-removed process?'

Seventeen years on, the shame was complete: I was turning my work from one language into the other without acknowledging it as such – in order to increase my chances of getting it published – and without daring to give credit to my originals when including them in my list of publications.

It was not until recently, when I began to look at the history of self-translation, that I became conscious of the fact that, traditionally, self-translation has indeed been surrounded by a sense of shame, largely inflicted on it by the critics and theorists of the day. In 1813, Friedrich Schleiermacher, for example, reduced the bilingual writer to nonentity by pronouncing that '[W]riting in a foreign language is never original... [If] in defiance of nature and morality, a writer becomes a traitor to his native language by surrendering himself to another... he can no longer move about in that language' (Walsh Hokenson and Munson 2007, 142). This insistence on the purity of language came from Schleiermacher's notion of 'One Country, One Language' (Walsh Hokenson and Munson 2007, 143), which found prominence – although, admittedly, after suffering some transformations – in Pauline Hanson's 'One Nation': an obsolete idea, and yet strangely persistent.

As recently as 2002, self-translation was condemned as 'an activity without content, voided of all the rich echoes and interchanges I have so far attributed to the practice of translation', and its practice was described as 'never innocent' because it 'occurs in situations of exile or of crude subjugation, where one language is attempting to take the place of another' (Whyte 2002, 69). It is true that I engaged in the act of self-translation 'in exile' but there is nothing

---

and 'Untitled' (I take you), in *Tirra Lirra* 5(3) (Autumn): 1995, 5; 'Song for an Exile', in *Overland* (September): 1994, 8 and in Denmark in *Kunapipi*, 16 (2): 1994, 49–52; 'Summer Night', 'Loneliness' and 'Mid-autumn Festival', in *Southern Review* (March): 1994, 99–100; 'A Blind Fortune-teller Tells Me That', in *Westerly* 39 (3): 1994, p. 89; 'Life', in *Tirra Lirra* 5 (1): 1994, 17; 'Untitled' (I hate spring), in *Narcissus* 10: 1994, 6; 'Dusk in Shanghai', 'About Poetry' and 'Untitled' (The nightingales have stopped singing, too), in *Poetry Monash* 43: 1994, 8–9; and 'Spring at Kingsbury, Melbourne', in *Antipodes* (June): 1994, 14, and in *Kunapipi* XV(3): 1993, 35–40.

wrong with using one language 'to take the place of another' if its purpose is the creation of a second life. A self-translator does no more than that promoted by the slogan, 'Freedom or Death'; his matching slogan would be 'Self-translation or Death'.

Whether 'innocent' or not – a nonsensical accusation in itself – self-translation has persisted throughout the ages, with such prominent practitioners as Rabindranath Tagore, Samuel Beckett, Joseph Brodsky, Ngũgĩ wa Thiong'o, Vladimir Nabokov, Czesław Miłosz and Julien Green. Self-translation is a constant need for more than just linguistic and literary survival. It is a process of adaptation and expansion in Nabokov's case; of living the languages in Green's case; and of challenging the languages in Beckett's case (Walsh Hokenson and Munson 2007, 168–200). In my case, though, it is a process of restoring self-confidence, of giving birth to myself, to my linguistic and literary self, in a second language, now equally my first, when no-one else shows interest in doing so. Against Whyte's claim that 'the person least qualified to translate any poem is the person who wrote it' (2002, 68), who better is there to translate – to trans-write – one's own work than oneself?

Two years after my arrival in Australia in April 1991, I wrote a poem in English titled 'Translating Myself' (Ouyang 1995a), presented below to give a sense of how the concept first geminated for me as a poet who self-translates:

'Translating Myself'

translating myself into English

as if I were a language

but am I not Chinese

am I not that ancient language that

resembles myself that is myself that is the birthmark on my face that makes you

comment to your friends without even looking

that he is Chinese or dismiss him

as a bloody Chink or Chow or burst into

Ching Chong Chinaman rhyme...

but translating myself is a problem

I mean how can I turn myself into another language

without surrendering myself

without betraying myself

without forgetting myself

without forgiving myself

without even losing myself in a different con/text

I mean how can English be so transparent

as not even to be able to hide my china-skinned identity

I mean how can a language be so indestructible that

it remains itself while being turned into another

or is this body of mine really two bodies

one English the other Chinese

translating myself is but re/creating

myself with languages or bodies

a discourse between two knowing halves

or wholes each the interpreter of the other

but this awareness of what is being written in another language

this awareness of what is being concealed in what is being translated

given up for gained or lost or both

this helpless feeling of subjection to a bilingual

force moving in between

translating myself I get double paid

by imagination and twice removed from the original

in the mind and on the paper

doing a simultaneous translation of myself

like having a simultaneous orgasm

both in your body and in your head

easy in the mirror

except for the awareness of the thing in between

but I translate myself

from Chinese into English

disappear into appearance

of another existence

looking back across the barrier of tied tongues

at the concealed image of the other body

Briefly, it can be said that self-translation is a necessity because the author-translator can only engage in it while he or she is still alive. William Shakespeare cannot translate himself because he died long ago; he is thus consigned to the fate of being forever translated by others. Self-translation is, therefore, an activity with as much worth as that of creation and self-creation.

My attempts at self-translation also include fiction. *The Eastern Slope Chronicle* (Ouyang 2002), my first full-length novel, has a number of paragraphs of translation rendered by a fictional character. It is actually based on a self-translation of my first book of fiction written in Chinese, which I self-published in 1999. One paragraph – an example of an early translation that is far from mature, but which contains a rawness that disappeared when my command of English improved – goes like this:

> Yes, this age is too fast. Nothing is lasting: love, friendship, life. Education starts from the womb, moving down from age five. To be in the thirties is to be old. To be in the fifties is to be trash. To be in the seventies is to be a corpse. I have now reached the middle age. What have I not experienced? At the age of eight or nine, I saw with my own eyes bloodbath, running like rivers. (Ouyang 2002, 339)

Elsewhere, such self-translation attempts have not met with much success. Apart from two short stories I wrote in Chinese and translated into English (Ouyang 1997; Ouyang 1995b), I have not had any luck with a novella, written in Chinese in China in 1987, self-translated many years later in Australia, and presented as such a few years ago. This has left me under the impression that self-translated works are still under-valued in Australia, although it may have something to do with the limited journal space allocated to fiction; after all, I have had poems published in the category of self-translation since 2008.[2]

A sub-genre of self-translation is what I call semi-self-translation, or collaborative self-translation, or, in John Kinsella's words, 'trans-version'.[3] Vladimir Nabokov is known to have sought assistance from his wife and son as 'sub-translators', to literally translate his works into English for him to work on in more depth (Walsh Hokenson and Munson 2007, 181). In providing the following 'trans-version' of one of my poems, Kinsella relied on the three elements I gave him: a brief idea of what the poem is about; the transliteration of the poem and the poem itself in Chinese, ie the sound; and the image. I'll start with the Chinese poem:

《激情一种》

那时，一种激情犹如创痛

电击了他的肉体

他不由自主地激动颤动悸动颠动乃至飘动浮动

在另一个肉体之上

他体会了一条鱼

临死前的所有表现

仿佛从透明中观望了

那根贯穿鱼体的黑线的中断

然后把嘴中涌出的所有唾液

收回

---

2   These self-translated poems are as follows: 'When a poet is forgotten', 'Fallen leaves', 'The story', 'Girl, unfamiliar girl, I love you, I love you', 'I hate spring' and 'The romance of a small town' in *Fires Rumoured about the City: Fourteen Australian Poets*, Macau: Association of Stories in Macau: 2009, 30–39; and 'Romance of a small town' and 'Girl, unfamiliar girl, I love you, I love you' in *Overland* 191: 2008, 77–78.

3   This term was first mentioned by Kinsella in emails to the author.

Translated by John Kinsella as follows:

'Ardour'

Also, I divide along the line,

want to arrive swiftly

with light shining through to a depth we cohabitate –

plimsoll, lateral, fish lines to keep

us upright in water cold

as heat, refulgent

and opaque; through it all

I dart, I lengthen my stroke, slice

through turbulence with my fins wide wide

awake. (Ouyang 2008)

It is amazing how close Kinsella managed to get to my original poem in spirit, without knowing what each Chinese character meant. My self-translation of the same poem follows:

'Passion'

Then, passion, like pain

Struck his body like electricity

He couldn't help being excited trembling shivering vibrating even floating drifting

Above another body

He was experiencing all

The expressions of a fish before it dies

Feeling as if he was watching through the transparency

The breakage of the black line going across the fish's body

Before he retrieved

All the phlegm that had surged to his mouth

In self-translation, the translator-author may inadvertently play the role of censor. One of the earliest poems I wrote in Australia was 'Sex Notice', which began with these two lines: 'I have come to this country for 90 days / 90 days without a fuck' (Ouyang 2005, 16). When the poem, self-translated into Chinese, subsequently appeared in a USA-based Chinese-language literary journal, the specific word 'fuck' was changed to gan, or 'do'[4] and the poem was published under a pseudonym. The fear that gripped me when I dealt with Chinese culture in the early days can clearly be seen. In fact, I had one Chinese poem published in my first collection of Chinese poetry minus its second half because it contained the word *shouyin* (masturbation) (Ouyang 1998, 38–39).

On the other hand, self-translation grants a great degree of freedom, linguistically if not politically. In the aforementioned collection, I translated my poem 'Moon over Melbourne' into Chinese, and rendered the ending lines, 'dreading so bloody dreading to see / the bloody bastard moon' (Ouyang 2005, 68), as '*haipa bloody haipa*', with the two Chinese characters sandwiching the word 'bloody', which I decided to leave in English to create a sense of the particular, language-grounded experience that the poem describes (Ouyang 1998, 83).

Whatever else it is, self-translation is a worthwhile endeavour in which authors take their past into their own hands and turn it into their future, watching their life blooming in a foreign language without the expedient of a third party. If authors ever want to give birth to the self, self-translation is a way to do so, provided they are equipped with at least two languages – and two hopes.

Postscript

As I reached the end of the writing of this chapter, I made a discovery: a poetry manuscript titled 'Translating Myself', an unpublished collection that I started compiling at the end of 1998 but left on an old computer,

---

4   Zuo Yu, 'xing de gaoshi' (Sex Notice), *xin dalu shi shuangyue kan* (*New World Poetry Bimonthly*) [USA], 29, August 1995, page number not recorded. This poem was written in English shortly after my arrival in Australia in April 1991, and was subsequently self-translated into Chinese and submitted for publication in 1995. The original English version was published in my first English poetry collection, *Moon over Melbourne and Other Poems* (Smythesdayle, Australia: Papyrus Publishing: 1995, 59–61). In 2005, when *Moon over Melbourne* was republished in the UK, 'Sex Notice' was again included.

where it remained until I went to it in search of other material. It is a book manuscript that I forgot about for over 10 years!

With this new discovery, new issues arise. For example, one poem that exists in its entirety in English is found to be minus a stanza in Chinese. To compensate for my vain efforts in finding it, I decided to give it a second rendering by self-translating it back into Chinese from the self-translated English stanza. This is something that I would not have envisaged in the early days and something I would not have been able to do if I were dead. In this sense, self-translation, ultimately, is a grace-saving, poetry-saving and life-saving exercise that authors must engage in before it is too late.

References

Meng Zhaoyi; Li Zaidao (eds). 2005. *Zhongguo fanyi wenxue shi* ('A History of Literary Translation in China'). Beijing: Peking University Press.

Ouyang Yu. 1995a. 'Translating Myself'. *Going Down Swinging*: 62–64.

Ouyang Yu. 1995b. 'The Wolves from the North'. In *Australian Short Stories* 52: 29–35.

Ouyang Yu. 1997. 'The White Cockatoo Flowers' Self-translated. In *Influence*, edited by Skrzynecki, Peter. Sydney: Transworld Publishers: 171–179.

Ouyang Yu. 1998. *Moerben zhi xia (Summer in Melbourne)*. Chongqing: Chongqing Publishing House.

Ouyang Yu. 2002. *The Eastern Slope Chronicle*. Blackheath, NSW: Brandl & Schlesinger.

Ouyang Yu. 2005. *Moon over Melbourne and Other Poems*. UK: Shearsman Books.

Ouyang Yu. 2008. 'Ardour'. *Jacket* 35. Trans. John Kinsella. Accessed 4 May 2012. Available from: http://jacketmagazine.com/35/yu-tb-kinsella.shtml.

Whyte, Christopher. 2002. 'Against self-translation'. *Translation and Literature* 11 (1) (Spring): 64–71. Accessed 21 October 2011. Available from: http://www.jstor.org/stable/40339902.

Walsh Hokenson, Jan; Munson, Marcella. 2007. *The Bilingual Text*. Manchester: St Jerome Publishing.

Chapter 5

Effective self-translation

How not to completely lose yourself in another's language

Lia Hills

For the purposes of this chapter, I ask the reader to indulge me a little in my use of the term 'self-translation' as I move away from the literal meaning of translating one's own work into another language, and conduct a more phenomenological investigation of the interplay between translation and writing, of the rapport that forms between one's own work and that of the other.

Recently, as part of my research for a novel about trauma, love and the mind–body problem, I followed one of the summer school classes offered by the Melbourne School of Continental Philosophy, 'Phenomenology meets the Neurosciences'. One of the lectures focused on the self and other in an approach to consciousness; the emphasis veered away from a Cartesian questioning of whether we can know if other minds even exist towards a more relational view of the self, and our sense of it, as being inter-subjective and connected to others. I found this new model to be especially fitting with regard to my work as both a writer and a translator, and propose that it is through contact with the language of the other that we begin to get a greater sense both of ourselves as writers and of our own work, particularly when engaging in translation.

Entering into translation is like entering into a relationship. It is a delicate balance between one's own language and the other's; cultures and nuance; meaning and subtext; rhyme and rhythm; and the time when the text was written and when the translation is read. When translating, the translator enters a process of deciding which of these factors are most important – to the translator, to the integrity of the work – and in translating each new author, the translator must begin another relationship and discover a new dynamic.

It is, of course, easier for the writer to translate into her mother tongue than the other way around, but both present her with opportunities to investigate the ways in which she works with language. Whether the writer translates her own work into a 'foreign' language or works side-by-side with the person doing so, the writer must discern her own voice in that language – must effectively reencounter that voice – which can facilitate the identification of certain idiosyncrasies or tendencies in the writer's practice that may otherwise have proved elusive. For example, I became increasingly aware of how important ambiguity is to me in my writing, whether that be in the form of a word having the potential for multiple meanings, or a line break in a poem allowing for various interpretations.

Translating one's work, or having it translated, also encourages the writer to 'fight' for certain aspects of style and approach, and, in the process, to identify priorities. I remember the conversation I had with a woman who was translating a poem of mine for inclusion in the Festival franco-anglais de poésie in Paris, and the associated journal, *La Traductière*. Generally the discussion went something like this: 'For me, maintaining the internal rhyme plus the dynamics inherent in the sound of the word are more important here than a literal translation, so I think we should go with another word'. Eventually, after several emails, we came to the understanding that it was more important to the integrity of the source poem to maintain, for example, the metaphorical sense of the word 'cantilever' and the way it helped bridge ideas in terms of sound, than to incorporate the correct architectural term. What I decided not to do was to translate my poem myself and present this translation to her – although this was suggested – because a new work was being created, and she was its author. Of course, this letting go is not always an easy process.

In 2008, I participated in the Franco-Anglais Poetry Festival held in Melbourne in partnership with the Parisian festival. In the workshops, it became increasingly clear that there was a divide between the Australian and French poets in their approach to translating the poems we discussed, poems that had been written by the poets present. The Australians almost invariably argued in defence of rhythm and maintaining the 'sense' of the poem, whereas the French tended towards a more 'correct' translation, each word generally translated in its most literal sense. In the defence of poetic features over literality, I felt a greater sense of the poets attempting to incorporate their own presence and their way of engaging with language within the translated work.

A few years ago, I was asked to write a libretto for a ballet to be performed in Switzerland, as well as accompanying poems, in French, that would be recorded and played over the music during the performance. My first instinct was to write the poems in English, with the intention of translating each one later into French, but as I started to translate one of the poems I found that not only was I diverging from the original work in a way in which I never would nor could if I were translating another writer's work, but that it felt increasingly like an unnatural process. It was then that I decided that it would be much better to write the poems directly in French, as I was forming a new relationship with the French language and its idiosyncrasies that was quite different from working with English. French rhymes much more readily than English and I found myself resisting this at first, often unsuccessfully; in the end I allowed a greater degree of rhyme at the end of lines than I ever had. This, in turn, forced me to look more closely at my use of rhyme in English, which tends to focus on internal rhyme. I then translated some of the poems back into English to see how they would work. What I discovered was that what I'd written was quite different to my work in English, and that I needed to rework the poems in French to better 'translate' my style and poetic tendencies. I had become somehow lost in the language, and though as a writer I am used to losing myself in language, and find this an essential part of how I work, I was experiencing this in a new and confronting way.

The poems in French were well received by the producers of the ballet despite my early uncertainties and, in the end, I found that I was able to not only give myself up to this notion of another 'self' emerging within the context of writing in another language, but also to learn from it as a writer. I effectively tapped into my French side. Most who go through the process of learning another language experience that similar phenomenon of being immersed in that language in such a way that they begin to dream in it, to see the world through it, to the point where their sense of self is briefly, or maybe permanently, altered.

I came to translation through what these days would be considered a more traditional route. Though I have always had a love of languages, particularly French, it was my desire to further my skills as a writer, and also to engage more intimately with the language of other writers, that drew me into an increasingly in-depth relationship with the French language and the possibilities offered by the act of translation, rather than any academic interests.

Poets have a long tradition of translating poetry or incorporating translations into their work, from Jack Kerouac, who helped popularise the modern haiku in the USA, to TS Eliot, who used extracts from works in other languages in *The Waste Land*, to Ezra Pound, whose 'creative translations' of works from languages such as French and Chinese raise vital questions about the nature of translation, especially when undertaken by a writer. Pound was essentially looking for, as he said, what 'could not be lost by translation' (Pound 1954, 77), as if seeking out some central core in poetry across nations and languages. Translation would continue to inform his work for the rest of his life and was intricately connected to his process of creation.

I began translating poetry when I was writing a verse novel and was dissatisfied with the translations of Apollinaire that I was referring to in the text. I was hearing something else than what the translator had put on the page – Apollinaire sounded different to me – and so I began. I also translate poetry that I cannot find translations of, or when I am requested to do a specific translation, for example, a recent piece in a Norton collection of Anglo-Saxon poems, *The Word Exchange* (Delanty and Matto 2011), translated by poets from around the world. But more and more, I translate poems that I think will inform my work. Some, like Pierre Alferi's poems from his collection *Kub Or* (Alferi 1994), I translated as much for the unusual use of line breaks he employed as for the incredible challenge that they presented – each poem 7 lines of 7 syllables. Such technical difficulty, I find, forces me to investigate my own language on a deeper level, to search harder for the rhythms and meanings I need, to overthrow old habits and find ways to communicate what is core in a piece, even if that means letting go of standard syntax and punctuation. In reading Alferi, sometimes I felt like I needed to learn how to breathe again. The collection had previously been translated into English, and although I quite liked these translations, it was the intense engagement with his work, enabled by translating it myself, that gave a completely different dimension to my relationship with it. It was a bit like the difference between being told what somebody is like and actually meeting them.

In Alferi's *Kub Or* poems, he presents a brief image or idea that ends with an envoi rather than beginning with a title, in what reads like a post-modern homage to the French – or rather Occitan and Provençal – troubadourian tradition. To give an example, here are some of his poems in French, followed by my own translation:

autre symptôme alarmant

de négligence spatiale

sans fin la séance hélas

sans leur lenteur d'asiates

de poses naturelles

verbales à la rigueur

a la grâce du malaise

    tai chi

one more alarming symptom

of spatial negligence the

séance without end alas

without their asian slowness

of unnatural poses

so rigorously verbal

at the mercy of malaise

    tai chi

avant de plonger un kub

or maggi l'on se met en

état d'ébullition

ah c'est si ah que c'est ah

absorbant ces mots tampon

périodique à déplier

vite une autre un dernier vite

    envoi

before to plunge a stock cube

or maggi we fall into

a state of ebullience

ah it's so ah that it's ah

absorbent these tampon words

periodically unfurled

quick one more one last one quick

dispatch

After completing these translations, I was fascinated not only with the visuals of Alferi's poems – these small cubes – and his use of line breaks, but also the fact that the tantalising constraints of these kinds of poems somehow mirrored the act of translation itself, which, following Willis Barnstone, I like to refer to as 'dancing in chains', a phrase sometimes employed when referring to the rules and restrictions involved in the writing of haiku and Tang poetry. So I began work on a poem of my own, which I later incorporated into my collection, *the possibility of flight* (Hills 2008). In my poem, I decided to take the idea of seven further by using the seven deadly sins as a structural and thematic base; in keeping with Alferi's modern urban setting, I drew on television shows as the core subject matter. The poem is called 'Seven: TV' in Latin, and each seven-line stanza ends with an envoi, which is the name of one of the deadly sins.

Following this work on Alferi's poetry, I decided to experiment in a different way with the translation aspect of poetry, expanding on the notion that translation is a new act of creation. I took a well-known poem by Mallarmé, 'Coup de Dés' or 'Roll of the Dice', and translated it into English; then I began rearranging the words into a new work, in a way not dissimilar to some of the ideals of the French surrealists. I worked from the premise that the translated words were now my own – that it was not a case of appropriation, but rather adaptation. These words formed the first half of the poem that retained French openings to each stanza sampled from Mallarmé. The second part of the poem was based on selecting pieces of text from the introduction to the collection and incorporating translated quotes into a kind of poetic dissertation on Mallarmé's work, taking them beyond prose into poetry. The resulting poem – 'Translating Mallarmé' –

was as much about the act of translation, and my approach to this practice, as it was an attempt to find my own way poetically through his language.

In 2008, I was presented with my first opportunity to translate a novel when the publishers of my own fiction asked if I would be interested in translating Marie Darrieussecq's novel *Tom est mort* (2007), which had been released in France about six months prior and nominated for both the Prix Femina and the Prix Goncourt. Translating a novel is of course very different from translating poetry. There is the question of length, of sustaining style over hundreds of pages, and the whole issue of meaning is more central in a longer work that incorporates at least some elements of narrative. Then there is the question of maintaining core language across translations, and how the work will be received as part of the author's body of work by academics and other commentators, especially when the author is so highly regarded and important within the context of a current literary tradition. But in the end, these contingencies gave over to other more artistically important ones, and essentially this came down to the relationship between my language and hers.

Stylistically, Darrieussecq is very idiosyncratic: often the narrator is not named in her work, and the reader feels immersed in her use of language in a way more particular to poetry than prose, the experience of the novel is more about induced states than narrative. As a writer, I was highly attuned to the importance of these traits, but also to the necessity of maintaining my own voice if the work were to sound authentic, and this is where I adhere absolutely to the notion of translator as writer. Choices were often difficult: whether to prioritise a play on words over metaphor or meaning if it was impossible to retain all three, which often it was; or whether to sacrifice literal meaning when Darrieussecq used internal rhyme or repetition to connect imbedded ideas across sentences and paragraphs. At times I favoured form over meaning – the poet in me required this; her loose use of narrative allowed it. Darrieussecq also employs sequences of words that sound like other phrases in order to suggest further meanings that the reader intuits even if not picking up on them directly. This characteristic is intimately connected with her other practice as a Lacanian psychoanalyst – I did my best to retain the sequences, again often prioritising them over literal translation. And amidst all this, I endeavoured to find a way for our two languages to come together, and here I speak not of French and English, but of her dialect and mine – the different, and sometimes similar, ways in which we manipulate and immerse ourselves in words – otherwise the danger was that it would all dissolve into parody. I had to draw on all my skills as a writer to render hers as effectively as I could, and yet, at the same time, I needed to strike a balance between what often felt like two complimentary yet opposing forces, especially as I had recently written a novel that also dealt with grieving and had a strong sense of how I had handled similar themes and states. In the end, it was the writer in me that took the upper hand, not the translator, a technique that I discussed with Darrieussecq, who is also a translator. One of the greatest compliments I received when the work was finished was from a colleague who knows my writing intimately. She said: 'I hear her in there, but I also hear you'.

To return to my original suggestion about a more phenomenological approach to self-translation, what I am increasingly aware of is that by immersing the self in the language of others the writer can gain a greater sense of the self as an integral part of a community of language, and that possibly the most intimate way of engaging with other writers – at least in my experience – is to translate them. The key is not to lose oneself so totally in the other language as to be unable to effectively emerge from it, enriched, and with a greater sense of embodiment, of presence in one's own language.

References

Pound, Ezra. 1954. *The Literary Essays of Ezra Pound*. Edited by TS Eliot. London: Faber & Faber.
Delanty, Greg; Matto, Michael, eds. 2011. *The Word Exchange: Anglo-Saxon Poems in Translation*. New York: Norton.
Alferi, Pierre. 1994. *Kub Or*. Paris: Éditions P.O.L.
Hills, Lia. 2008. *the possibility of flight*. Brisbane: IP Publications.
Darrieussecq, Marie. 2007. *Tom est mort*. Paris: Éditions P.O.L.
Darrieussecq, Marie. 2009. *Tom Is Dead*. Trans. Lia Hills. Melbourne: Text Publishing.

Part II

Creative practice

Part II

Creative practice

Chapter 6

Between 'Aussies' and 'wah-sers'

Translating Alice Pung's *Unpolished Gem* into Italian

Adele D'Arcangelo

[Creative writers] are bound by all manners of constraints: political, social, poetic and linguistic, as well as the constraints of the text itself, which creates a context potentially confining and determining the form and meaning of every utterance... For in fact creativity is often intimately tied to constraint, it is a response to it, it is enhanced by it... Constraints in this sense can be seen as one of the main sources of creativity.

(Boase-Beier and Holman 1999, 6)

In this chapter I discuss some aspects of my translation of Alice Pung's best-selling Australian novel *Unpolished Gem*, considering which constraining elements – both in Pung's creative writing process and in my translation – represented challenges and pushed author and translator to creatively overcome the limits imposed by those constraints. The first part of my analysis focuses on the description of the editorial processes the book underwent in the original and target cultures, paying particular attention to the way editorial policies, shaped by economic and marketing strategies, can represent forms of constraint for authors. The chapter then underlines the main features of *Unpolished Gem* from the point of view of content and style. The critical reading will be supported by authors such as Homi Bhabha, Salman Rushdie and Hanif Kureishi, whose theories are particularly relevant to the concept of multicultural creative writing as a form of translation itself. These specific considerations hope to contribute to a better understanding of the difficulties the translator had to identify and how, in the final analysis, overcoming them could be considered a new form of creative re-writing within the theoretical framework that refers to translation as a process of 'transcreation' (Bassnett and Trivedi 1999).

Editorial policies and power in the translation process

Released in 2006 by independent Melbourne imprint, Black Inc., *Unpolished Gem* was warmly received by both readers and critics in Australia. The work has been reprinted twice, and early in 2007 won for Pung the Newcomer of the Year Prize at the Australian Book Industry Awards. Rights were then bought by Portobello, which distributed the book in the UK, North America and India, where again the book received critical acclaim. In 2009 the Italian publisher, Mobydick,[1] bought rights to an Italian translation of the book, which was issued in 2010 with the title *Gemma impura*.[2]

Unpolished Gem, narrated in the form of a memoir, is the story of a family rebuilding their lives in Australia after the horrific Pol Pot years. In the Portobello edition of the book, the author was asked to add a preface, in which she provides a historical account of Cambodian genocide, as well as a genealogy of her family. Neither element was present in the first edition of the book published by Black Inc., the independent Australian-based publisher. Operating with less concern for the commercially oriented policies and economic dynamics of mainstream publishing houses, Black Inc. accepted Pung's manuscript, presented in the form of short stories, and edited it with the author in order to shape it into a novel.[3]

The request to add a preface she had not intended to write was viewed as an imposition by Pung, who asked the Italian publisher Mobydick to ignore both the preface and the family tree on the front page of the Italian edition, even though the rights for that edition were bought from Portobello, not Black Inc. In a personal communication Pung told me she was not happy

---

1 Mobydick is based in Faenza, a town in Northern Italy near Bologna.
2 The equivalent of 'unpolished' in Italian would be '*grezza*', but this did not sound appealing enough to me or to the publisher. My choice was for '*impura*' (impure) because the original title is explained in a passage of the book where Alice, the protagonist, refers to a Cambodian saying about the cultural cliché of female virginity.
3 The first short stories were written by Alice Pung when she was 18 and the editing process was mainly intended to give them a sequential order that could work in novel form.

with Portobello's decision because she felt that it was a way of placing her novel within a literary trend, whereas she would have preferred not to be confined to a particular editorial niche. While it is certainly true that Portobello's preference for a 'familiar label' was a commercial strategy to sell more copies, the clear imposition on the creative writing process was overcome once the book moved into a new editorial market. This was possible because Mobydick, being itself a small, though well known, independent Italian publisher, was somehow more in line with the original spirit with which Black Inc. presented the memoir. Moreover, small publishers are usually more likely to encourage collaboration among authors, translators and editors and this is particularly rewarding for all parties involved, as is underlined by Bassnett and Bush:

> A collaborative project, either a translator working together with the source language writer or with other translators, turns out to be an important translational moment, displaying the richness of each subjectivity simultaneously, entering into relationships with the text and with language, creating intriguing intertextual configurations: collaborations ultimately allow us to see how all the people involved are all contributors, that is co-writers. (Bassnett and Bush 2006, 10)

Within the context of this specific mission, I must stress that Mobydick is particularly good at recognising the role of the translator as a 'co-writer'. In fact Guido Leotta, owner of Mobydick, makes a point of including the translator's name on the front cover of all his books. I would finally like to add that I had the great pleasure of collaborating with Alice Pung herself during all the phases of elaboration of my translation as well as during the editing process. This co-writing/translating experience also saw both author and translator present during all the events organised throughout Italy for the launch of the book, in November 2010.[4]

Many aspects related to economic and cultural power in editorial policies have been discussed by translation-studies theorists such as Lawrence Venuti, Umberto Eco and Susan Bassnett, and the promotional aspects of releasing a

---

4   This particular, unusual and very special cooperation experience for everybody involved in the Italian publication of the book was possible thanks to the enthusiasm and commitment of Prof. Rosa M. Bollettieri-Bosinelli (from the University of Bologna), who promoted most of the book-launch events and personally contacted Alice Pung about a possible project to translate her memoir, after meeting her for the first time during an International Association for Translation and Intercultural Studies conference held in Melbourne in 2009.

cultural product are also relevant to my analysis. In fact, although Pung did not feel perfectly at ease with the 'multicultural label' applied to her book, it is true that many reviews – both for the English and the Italian version of the book – placed it in this specific field and market, therefore also outlining an ideal target reader for the book, one who is interested in this specific kind of product, a particularly relevant element given that '... the translator... is always translating for somebody or some group of people. Even if there is not always a client, there is always a perceived consumer, a targeted reader within a community of readers, whose needs translators ignore at their peril' (Boase-Beier and Holman 1999, 11).

Unpolished Gem and Alice Pung's literary project: Identity, belonging and gender constraints

Alice, known to her Chinese-Cambodian family as Agheare (Good News), is a child of refugees. In her memoir Pung shifts effortlessly from the world of her family – where her mother speaks little English, and her father becomes a businessman and takes up a Retrovision franchise – to the world of school and university, where she tries to adopt the values of a typical Australian teenager.

In a review by Deborah Bogle, Pung is reported describing *Unpolished Gem* as a distinctly 'Australian book' in that it celebrates small successes rather than grand achievements; but she nonetheless states that in the book 'there's also a particular migrant narrative where you struggle a lot to reach this thing called success in the end' (Bogle 2007, 13).

Asian-Australian writer is a definition of herself Pung might be willing to accept. This is certainly stressed by her second literary achievement, a collection of short stories and poems she edited, the title of which, *Growing up Asian in Australia*, is itself a kind of militant statement, underlining once again the importance of the concept of identity. As Pung puts it in her introduction to the collection:

> I hope that these loose themes will help bring to the forefront questions of identity, place and perspective. Because the stories deal so insightfully with the challenges of coming to terms with multiple identities, they move beyond crude labels such as 'bananas' and 'coconuts.' We are not fruit, we are people. These are not sociological essays, but deeply personal stories told with great literary skill. They show us not only

what it is like to grow up Asian in Australia, but also what it means to be an Asian-Australian. (Pung 2008, 2)

Both *Unpolished Gem* and *Growing Up Asian in Australia* are set texts in schools all over Australia, evidence of how Australian education and politics consider multicultural and identity issues and discourse crucial.[5] Following these two first books, Pung also published a third one in 2011, *Her Father's Daughter*, a new work narrated in diary form, in which Alice is once again the protagonist of a search for identity through an exploration of her father's background.

In *Unpolished Gem*, Pung tries to capture the two different yet overlapping and ultimately mingled dimensions of her life: the Australian- and Asian-ness. One initial aspect of this integration process is well expressed at the beginning of the book when the father, in naming his daughter Alice, actually evokes the Western story about a 'girl who finds herself in an enchanted land', wishing to give to his baby a name that her future legions of white friends would be able to remember and pronounce on the one hand, and with which Alice would feel at ease on the other: 'This new daughter of his will grow up in this WonderLand and take for granted things like security, abundance, democracy and the little green man on the traffic lights' (Pung 2006, 19). Although Pung deals with questions of plural identities and Otherness, celebrating exoticism is not the aim, of course, of her literary project; she is undeniably more interested in trying to capture the 'us' in the most universal sense, her identity embodying an Australianness that is rarely reflected on TV or radio but that is relatively common in ordinary everyday life (Bogle 2007).

When referring to his first literary successes, Hanif Kureishi remembers that the cultural world and the media started showing interest for what was then dubbed 'New Britain': 'They required stories about the new British communities, by cultural translators, as it were, to interpret one side to the other' (Ranasinha 2001, 12). The same cultural dynamic may well underpin the great success Alice Pung enjoyed with her first novel, and the fact that she is now often grouped with authors who seem to be fulfilling the same need in Australia. Interestingly enough, Kureishi refers to the concept of 'cultural translators' in his critical work; and in fact Alice Pung is the classic migrant child whose immersion in two cultures makes her ideally placed to become an interpreter. Like Asian-British writers, Pung favours the autobiographical

---

5   Alice Pung herself is also often called to give talks on multicultural issues in schools or at special multicultural celebration events.

form to express the unease felt by the children of immigrants. She therefore offers a global view of the world of childhood and adolescence, two phases of life that are themselves always troubled by transformation and instability. During their childhood and teenage years, second-generation migrants discover through direct experience that they are living discrimination in classrooms and playgrounds, and thus become conscious of their cultural dislocation (Buonanno 2009). And this is what actually happens to Alice: 'I woke up one morning with a false skin on my face. The skin was made of rubber, and it took a great effort to move the muscles... I could not prise off this rubber death mask. I felt a funeral in my brain, and we hadn't even studied Emily Dickinson yet'[6] (Pung 2006, 177). In many of these literary works the experience of migration and of dislocation is described as harder for women, who often live a shadowy existence in which especially the mothers of the newcomers are never able to completely adapt. Accepting integration is difficult for them and this is even more evident in the Chinese culture in which Alice grew up at home, crushed between the opposing personalities of her mother and paternal grandmother.

In Pung's telling, children and women are those who suffer the most: desperation runs like a bloodline through the female characters. As Anna Goldsworthy points out: 'Pung paints a bleak portrait of her mother's depression, and that of a generation of Asian women, sitting in their 'double-storey brick-veneer houses', paralysed by luxury. It is a *Feminine Mystique* suburban nightmare, made more claustrophobic by language'[7] (Goldsworthy 2006, 7). Yet when invited to the 2008 Multicultural Women's Day, Alice Pung gave a speech in which her blunt description of her mother's life also expressed a considerable tribute:

> I wrote a book about three generations of women in my family – my mother, my grandmother and myself... There are hundreds and thousands of migrant women like my mother in this country, who are invisible to outside society because they don't know English. They are only visible in their own communities, or even just their own homes. People say that migrant women like myself are successful because we have made it to the outside world. But I am only here because someone

---

6   The clear ironic element, a significant aspect of Alice Pung's creative project, will be discussed later in this chapter.

7   Goldsworthy is referring to Betty Friedan's seminal feminist text *The Feminine Mystique*, which was first published in 1963. *The Feminine Mystique* interrogates the insidious expectation that all women find complete fulfilment in the role of mother and housewife.

invested in my education. Someone spent all their pay on a good school for me. Someone cooked meals for me so I would not have to take time from study, someone drove me to school without being able to read street-signs… Migrant women have always invisibly, silently worked hard so that the next generation – women like myself – will not be invisible, so that we can have some degree of recognition in the world. (Pung, online)

It seems to me that in her work Alice Pung is definitely describing her own personal experience as representative of a social- and gender-based larger experience within the Asian/Chinese-Australian community. But what is peculiar about Alice Pung's style is that she describes the experience of being a daughter of refugees with the cheerfulness typical of her young age. Pung started writing the short stories that were then collected in *Unpolished Gem* at the age of 18. If her story is a story of successful integration, as it is, this is particularly stressed by a distinctive feature of her style, namely, her ability to laugh at her own miseries as well as at her family's strange cultural idiosyncrasies; and this is something that Pung owes specifically to the 'Western side' of her identity.

Giving due importance to specific aspects of Alice Pung's writing was essential to my analysis and interpretation of her work, and laid the basis for the main choices I made when deciding translation strategies, given that translation can be considered a form of literary criticism in the first place (Bassnett and Bush 2006, 7). Moreover, the particularly fresh and youthful voice we can appreciate when reading Pung's book actually constituted an element of constraint for me, because there is a generational gap between her and me. When defining this as the 'peculiar touch' she gave to her writing, I also had to work on the tone of my translation so as to make the Italian version sound as young, fresh and playful as the original. This was the main constraining challenge I had to face because, as stressed by Lakshmi Holmström: 'the translator too is gendered and operates from his or her own cultural assumptions and relationships. He or she cannot be an impersonal or transparent conduit' (Holmström 2006, 43).

The Asian-Australian manipulation of the English language

Pung's style has been defined as an 'easy and colloquial voice, which has a peculiar accent and a distinctive rhythm that perhaps stems from the Teochow dialect of her childhood' (Goldsworthy 2006, 7). *Unpolished Gem* is a perfect expression of the retelling and rewriting possibilities afforded by metropolitan/multicultural English to 'in-between identities writers' (Buonanno 2009, 126).

What is made possible in multicultural writing is a never-ending process of translation as manipulation and recreation of the English language itself, thanks to writers who are themselves cultural mediators and translators. One of the strategies to somehow 'desacralize' the hegemonic usage of the language (Bhabha 1994) is the constant code switching technique that Pung's ironic style allows. Salman Rushdie underlines that the process of transformation that the English language undergoes is thanks to the contribution of writers who belong to different cultures: 'What seems to me to be happening is that those peoples who were once colonised by the language are now rapidly remaking it, domesticating it, becoming more and more relaxed about the way they use it – assisted by the English language's enormous flexibility and size, they are carving out large territories for themselves within its frontiers' (Rushdie 1981, 64). On page 94 of her book, Pung, referring to her mother, writes: 'She could not read because she had been housebound for two decades. And now, over the dinner table, she would watch as my father and his children littered their language with English terms, until every second word was in a foreign tongue' (Pung 2006, 94). This last quote is a useful starting point for a consideration of specific stylistic and linguistic features of this work, but before coming to this I will briefly consider the setting of Pung's memoir: Melbourne, and in particular, Melbourne suburbs such as Footscray and Braybrook. The metropolitan area itself emerges as a space that is particularly open to the experience of retelling, and rewriting: 'The city is itself the multiform space, whose multiform elements symbolise and prepare for further transformations and stratifications of experiences' (Duncan et al. 2004, 56).

Duncan, Leigh, Madden and Tynan in their sociological analysis *Imagining Australia: Ideas for Our Future* argue that the real achievement has taken place in the Australian suburbs. It is ordinary Australians, they say, with their fundamental sense of tolerance, decency and willingness to give newcomers a fair go, who have lived side by side with wave after wave of new migrants and have made multiculturalism work. And it is in this suburban Australia – perfectly familiar to Alice Pung – that the creative cultural and linguistic encounter takes place:

This suburb, Footscray, has possibly the loudest and grottiest market in the Western world, although that term doesn't mean much when you're surrounded by brown faces... This is the suburb where words like *and*, *at* and *of* are redundant, where full sentences are not necessary. 'Two kilo dis. Give me seven dat.' If you were to ask politely 'Would you please be so kind as to give me a half kilo of the Lady Fingers' the shop-owner might not understand you. 'You wanna dis one? Dis banana? How many you want hah?' (Pung 2006, 3)

In *Unpolished Gem* English appears more than ever as a language 'on the move', able to permeate and capture other tongues' influences, hence enhancing the polyphonic character of Pung's narrative. The author moulds the language to her needs, therefore readers will hear Asian men and women speaking broken English at the market, or Asian-Australian children trying to learn the new tongue. They will read passages written in English but describing old Chinese people's view of the world and therefore sounding like an English translation of a Chinese Teochew dialect dialogue.

The flexibility of the English language, therefore, contributes to the definition of a 'third space' in writing; its capacity to assimilate the 'new' becomes an instrument in the process of the broadening of borders (Buonanno 2009). This broadening is the aim of literary works such as Alice Pung's memoir, which itself becomes responsible for projecting Australian literature towards a progressive internationalisation.

'The undefined and indefinable space between source language and target language'

As stressed by Bassnett and Bush, 'the paradoxical condition of translators is to inhabit in-betweenness, and more precisely the undefined – and undefinable – space between SL and TL' (Bassnett and Bush 2006, 8). The concept of the liminal space created by multicultural literary works in which different identity perspectives overlap has also been discussed, together with the concept of translation as 'in-betweeness', by authors such as Homi Bhabha and Salman Rushdie. From this standpoint, then, I now move on to consider the defining features of Pung's style, how they underpin her work as a whole, and how I decided to render those elements in the new 'third space' that my Italian translation of *Unpolished Gem* created.

In terms of the (in)visibility of the translator, I decided not to use any extra-textual elements, such as an introduction, footnotes or a glossary, first of all because I knew this would not have been accepted or appreciated by Pung, and also because Italian readers might well have become somewhat more familiar with this kind of fiction. Thus I felt it would have been too traditional an approach and hence inappropriate to the aims of my translation, given the kind of target reader I envisaged. In Italy we do have a growing, though still small, corpus of Italian migrant literature (especially from young second-generation African-Italian authors), and a number of books have been translated from multicultural English. In order to make myself 'visible as a translator' (Venuti 1995), I attempted to 'force' the target language a little, with strategies aimed at trying to recreate Pung's versatile style, especially the element I would define as 'creative estrangement'.

Use of code-switching and Chinese terms: The creative estrangement effect

In the following example of code-switching, I decided to maintain instances of non-standard spoken English exactly as it was written in the original:

> When they haggle over the price of trotters, there is much hand gesticulating and furrowing of brow because the parties *do not spik da Inglish velly good*. 'Like a chicken trying to talk to a duck' my mother calls these conversations. (Pung 2006, 13)
>
> *Quando si contratta il prezzo dei piedini di maiale c'è un gran agitarsi di mani e aggrottare di sopracciglia perché le parti* do not spik da Inglish velly good. *"Come un pollo che cerca di parlare a un'anatra", così mia madre definisce quelle conversazioni.* (Pung 2010, 12)

In another code-switching example, I deemed it more appropriate to incorporate non-standard Italian usage because, while the previous example would have been understandable for my ideal target reader, given that it is the first phrase with which English-language learners become familiar, in the more complex passage below my intention was to experiment with the language to recreate the polyphony of accents at the marketplace, and to see if Italian could sound, in Rushdie's words (1981), as flexible and permeable as English:

This is the suburb where words like *and*, *at* and *of* are redundant, where full sentences are not necessary '*Two kilo dis. Give me seven dat.*' If you were to ask politely 'Would you please be so kind as to give me a half kilo of the Lady Fingers' the shop-owner might not understand you 'You wanna dis one? Dis banana? How many you want hah?' (Pung 2006, 3)

Questa è la periferia dove particelle come e, a e di sono ridondanti, dove le frasi complete non sono necessarie. "Due chili questo. Dai sette quello". Volendo essere così educati da chiedere con cortesia "Per favore, le dispiace darmi mezzo chilo di banane", il venditore potrebbe non capire "Vuoi questa? Questa banana? Quante banane, hah?" (Pung 2010, 12)

All the Chinese expression or words that were present in the original have been maintained in the translation:

'*Ta ku le*' said the hairdresser to my mother in Mandarin when my parents came to pick me up. She has been sooking.

Ta ku le - disse la parrucchiera a mia madre in mandarino quando i miei genitori vennero a prendermi. Ha pianto.

Phonetic transcriptions of the kinds of non-standard English pronunciation likely to be used by an Asian speaker have been maintained and/or adapted with strategies appropriate to the situation and context described:

phon phon > *plonto plonto*[8]

computah > *computah*

escooose mi plis I nid to go to da toylit > *scusa pel favole, posso andale in bagno?* (instead of '*scusa per favore posso andare in bagno*')

The last example is particularly significant because it shows how the very act of recreating the migrants' discourse embodies their struggle to integrate. When she was a small child, Alice was ashamed of asking her teacher to go to the toilet because she realised she did not 'sound' like the other children when speaking English. As a result, she always went home with

---

8 Considering the difficulty some Asian people have in pronouncing the 'r' sound, I decided to translate 'phon' (telephone) using the substandard '*plonto*' (instead of '*pronto*'), the Italian equivalent of 'Hello' when answering a telephone call.

wet trousers, until her teacher finally forced the small girl to pronounce what was a 'taboo question' for her. The strategies used for the phonetic transcription of an Asian speaking English are mingled with nicknames and interjections that combine to increase the effect of estrangement for the source language reader. The following examples illustrate how I once again attempted to recreate a similar effect for the target language reader with strategies of phonetic transcription (example 1) and creative ironic elements (example 2):

> 1) exclamations mostly expressing surprise (wah) or pain (woe, aiyoo etc.)
>
> wah, woe, aiyoo, aiyah, oyah... > *wah, woe, ahiuh, ahiah, ohiah...*
>
> 2) the creative ironic element
>
> Horseface > *Cavallona* (Big Female Horse)
>
> Toothless Aunt > *Zia Sdentata*
>
> Duck Brother > *Fratello Papero*
>
> Big Fat Potato > *Faccia da Tubero* (Tuber/Yam Face)
>
> Round Red-haired Demon > *Demone dal testone rosso* (Big-Red-haired Demon)[9]

At one level the above examples, and many others in the original work and in the translation, create an effect of estrangement that permeates the entire text, while they also shape the source and target languages into a new form to which readers gradually grow accustomed. A perfect example of the estrangement effect which in fact fuses English and Chinese in a way that embodies the linguistic and cultural integration process is represented by the term 'wah-ser', a neologism Pung invented to convey how fascinated and surprised her parents and relatives were by the abundance and variety of goods available in Australia. Italian is not as flexible and compressed as a language, therefore I tried to stress the ironic dimension here and to try to convey, as far as possible, these people's astonishment by defining them as *'Esclamatori di Wah'* (Wah declaimers).

---

9   With 'Horseface' Pung is referring to an aunt of hers, while 'Round Red-haired Demon' is the nickname her family gave to her cousin's Australian husband. These are all translation into English of the equivalent Chinese nicknames.

Translation and recreation of new cultural spaces

I only occasionally adopted strategies of amplification or explication of the text in order to avoid introducing footnotes and to help readers by using a slight degree of domestication, mainly for culture-specific items:

> This is the suburb of madcap Franco Cozzo and his polished furniture
>
> *Questa è la periferia di quel burino di Franco Cozzo e dei suoi mobilifici*
> *straluccicanti*

Here I described Franco Cozzo as a '*burino*' (a Roman dialect word meaning 'snazzy') and explained that Franco Cozzo owns furniture shops.[10]

Below are examples of how I used amplification to describe product brands, though it was impossible to fully convey the significance and appeal that these extremely familiar products hold for Australian children:

> 1) I boiled some water for *Milo*, for my sisters >
>
> *Preparai due tazze di bevanda al malto* Milo *per le mie sorelle* (I prepared two mugs of malt drink Milo for my sisters)[11]
>
> 2) spearmint Wrigley > *cicca alla menta* Wrigley (spearmint Wrigley chewing gum)

Where readers could infer the meaning of Chinese, Cambodian or Australian unknown words or products from the context, I did not add any explanation but left all references to Asian and/or Australian culture exactly as they occurred in the original, to gradually acclimatise the reader to the flavours and products of this new space:

> Aussies> aussies
>
> bancao > *bancao*

---

10 To decide how to render the adjective 'madcap' I asked Alice Pung what exactly she meant with it, if it was more unpredictable or snazzy/garish. She answered that it could mean both, but in this case it was definitely more the latter. I then also watched some of Franco Cozzo's TV commercials and how he was presented on the web, to find out that he was often listed in 'Trash TV' shows. Additionally, pictures of the furniture sold in his shops helped me in making this choice.

11 Italian children are used to drinking hot milk or camomile, but boiling water to prepare a drink for children is not a habit or expression Italians are familiar with. Instead, it would refer more to the act of making pasta.

blood gelly > *gelatina di sangue di maiale*

taro cakes > *frittelle di taro*

I adopted such translation strategies to re-create the novel character of the Asian-Australian English from which I translated. The underlying intention was to convey the permeability of the English language as described by Rushdie and to try, as far as possible, to mirror it in Italian.

There is a clear correspondence between the cultural contamination, the occupation of the third or liminal space, explored in Pung's work, and the concept of cultural translation formulated by critics and writers, who regard it as a paradigm of the processes of intercultural clashes or contacts. The function of authors–cultural translators such as Alice Pung is heightened by the use they make of the English language (in this case Australian-English), which they mould and manipulate in order to re-create and make other cultures echo and resound in it. The attention to both the linguistic and the cultural aspects involves other processes of contamination and hybridisation, made possible by the translation and reception of these works in other languages and cultures, hence opening further spaces for Australian multicultural creative writing and its international diffusion. Through and across cultural translation, writers and translators can therefore jointly plot a course able to outline Australian identities. What I hope potential Italian readers of *Gemma impura* will find is a flavour of Australian multicultural society, as well as a picture of the Chinese culture that has come to live next door in Italian cities, but about which we still know very little.

References

Bassnett, Susan; Bush, Peter, eds. 2006. *The Translator as Writer*. London: Continuum.
Bassnett, Susan; Trivedi, Harish, eds. *Postcolonial Translation: Theory and Practice*. London, New York: Routledge.
Bhabha Homi. 1994. *The Location of Culture*. London: Routledge.
Boase-Beier, Jean; Holman, Michael, eds. 1999. *The Practices of Literary Translation*. Manchester: St Jerome.
Buonanno Giovanna. 2009. 'Alcune considerazioni su la scrittura della black Britain tra ibridazione e traduzione culturale' In *Per una fenomenologia del tradurre*, edited by Nasi, Franco; Silver, Marc. Roma: Officina, 119–137.
Lakshmi Holmström. 2006. 'Let poetry win: The translator as writer – an Indian perspective'. In *The Translator as Writer*, edited by Bassnett, Susan; Bush, Peter. London: Continuum, 33–45.
Bogle, Deborah. 2007. 'God of Small Things'. *The Advertiser* (September 22, Books): 13.
Duncan, Macgregor; Leigh, Andrew; Madden, David; Tynan, Peter. 2004. *Imagining Australia: Ideas for Our Future*. Sydney: Allen & Unwin.

Goldsworthy, Anna. 2006. 'Flagrant act of word spreading'. *Australian Book Review* (7 November).

Pung, Alice, ed. 2008. *Growing up Asian in Australia*. Melbourne: Black Inc.

Pung, Alice. 2006. *Unpolished Gem*. Melbourne: Black Inc.

Pung, Alice. 2008. 'Multicultural women's day address'. [Internet]. Accessed 16 November 2011. Available from: http://alicepung.com/blog/wp-content/uploads/2007/10/multiculturalwomensfestival.pdf.

Pung, Alice. 2009. *Unpolished Gem*. London: Portobello.

Pung, Alice. 2010. *Gemma impura*. Trans. D'Arcangelo, Adele. Faenza: Mobydick.

Pung, Alice. 2011. *Her Father's Daughter*. Melbourne: Black Inc.

Ranasinha, Ruvani. 2001. *Hanif Kureishi*. Writers and their work series. London: Northcote House.

Rushdie, Salman. 1981. *Imaginary Homelands: Essays and Criticism 1981–1991*. London: Granata.

Venuti, Lawrence. 1995. *The Translator's Invisibility: A History of Translation*. London: Routledge.

Vieira, Else Ribeiro Pires. 1999. 'Liberating Calibans: Readings of antropofagia and Haroldo de Campos' *Poetics of Transcreation*'. In *Post-Colonial Translation: Theory and Practice*, edited by Bassnett, Susan; Trivedi, Harish. London and New York: Routledge: 95–113.

Chapter 7

What's so funny about that?

On translating (post)colonial humour – the case of

Moetai Brotherson's *Le Roi absent*

Jean Anderson

The translation of humour is a relatively unexplored aspect of literary translation studies: within this specialist area, critical works dealing with translating humour in (post)colonial texts, with one notable exception (Tymoczko 1999), are few and far between.[1] Considering some recent theoretical work on the translation of humour and on issues pertaining to postcolonial translation, this study will draw on examples from a current project, the translation of Moetai's Brotherson's *Le Roi absent*, to suggest possible solutions (and some of their implications) for specific types of humour, notably: word play; interlingual humour (code-switching and accents); humour and the erotic; and the use of juxtaposition.

In each of these cases, the translator may deploy a range of strategies, but should invariably keep in mind the context in which the source text originated. It is not my intention to determine procedures applicable in translating postcolonial humour generally, although some of the following discussion may well be applicable in other texts. I intend, rather, to focus on the use of humour in this work, and on the challenges it poses for the translator, who must in some circumstances be prepared not only to translate but also, in a sense, to rewrite.

---

1   Tymoczko's chapter on 'Translating the Humour in Early Irish Hero Tales' (191–221) is, however, largely very specific to the Irish situation. This is hardly surprising, since postcolonial studies were and are based on the need to recognise specificities in and differences between situations.

Although for more radical thinkers, French Polynesia is arguably not a *post*colonial society (its political representatives having voted in August 2011, albeit controversially, to request listing by the United Nations as a country in urgent need of decolonisation), it has obvious structural elements in common with both colonial and postcolonial societies. It is multicultural to a certain degree, notably as a result of Hakka Chinese immigration in the early twentieth century, and has a population that is predominantly (around 67 per cent) indigenous Polynesian; but, with a large percentage of positions of authority held by *Métropolitains* (French people), the country remains under the direct control of France in a number of core areas.[2] Thus any text by a French-Polynesian writer must be read in the context of this relationship between Oceanian islands and France *Métropolitaine*; all the more so when, as in the case of *Le Roi absent*, both indigenous and French settings and characters come into play. The humour in texts such as these may range across a number of categories, but it is rarely innocent. While translators will inevitably find creative solutions in dealing with these humorous elements, examining some of them in detail and within their context may lead to a more systematic identification of possible strategies.[3]

Le Roi absent: The (post)colonial context

Perhaps the most striking thing about Moetai Brotherson's *Le Roi absent* is its multiplicity, or even, somewhat tautologically, its many multiplicities. The story itself splits into two parts of approximately equal length, each with a different narrator-protagonist; the timeframe of each is shadowed by echoes from a number of different epochs, ranging from the distant past (prehistoric, pre-writing) to events of the sixteenth to twentieth centuries. Multiple eras and voices are woven together, evoking a diversity of other

2 Colonised in 1880, the islands known as French Polynesia became an Overseas Territory (*Territoire d'Outremer*) in 1946, an Overseas Collectivity (*Collectivité d'Outremer*) in 2004 and, in 2007, an Overseas Country (*Pays d'Outremer*), where the areas of justice, education, security and defence are still administered directly by France. It is now illegal to track ethnicities officially and the most recent figures date from 1988: 67 per cent Polynesian, 16 per cent mixed Polynesian/European/East Asian, 12 per cent European (mainly French) and 5 per cent East Asian (mainly Chinese).

3 Although we were unable to delve deeply into the range of humorous strategies used by Brotherson, some of the points covered in the following discussion were triggered by interactions that took place at the translation workshop held by Monash University in February 2011, and I would like to acknowledge here the stimulating contributions of the French workshop participants.

perspectives on, and narratives about and from, the Pacific: in that sense, the book is a sweeping introduction to the history of Oceania, as well as a combination of two 'biographical', character-centred narratives.

The author makes use of a great deal of humour in pulling together disparate elements, even when the underlying questions in this picaresque[4] epic are ostensibly of serious intent (What are the possible sources of Pacific settlement? How did the god of the Christian missionaries come to replace the powerful deities that preceded them? How is the Pacific represented in the accounts of European and indigenous storytellers? How do people make stories out of their environments, and indeed out of their own lives and the lives of those they meet? What is reality, and what is delusional fiction?).

In short, *Le Roi absent*, 'The Missing King',[5] is a deeply complex and highly appealing weaving together of the many strands of both its protagonists' and its implied readers' experiences. Much of the text will speak most clearly to a Pacific-based readership, in particular residents of French Polynesia and especially Tahiti (and in translation, to English-speaking Polynesian populations); however, in common with other fiction emerging from the French Pacific, it has been written (or at least published) in a kind of double perspective that aims simultaneously at both a French and a local public.[6] In addition, in *Le Roi absent*, Brotherson uses an initially naïve, presumably mildly autistic narrator (of whom I will mention more later), so that a certain degree of puzzlement and explanation is the norm in the opening narrative. These two factors can be readily exploited by readers unfamiliar with the setting to extract the necessary information to situate the story. At first sight, this may seem the antithesis of resistant (post)colonial literature, a process of 'writing for' rather than 'writing back'. However, I hope to show that once the use of humour is taken into account, the deeper, more radical engagement of Brotherson's novel, with its broad geographical and historical sweep, comes into sharper focus.

---

4   'Picaresque', as in a text 'in which the adventures of an engagingly roguish hero are described in a series of usually humorous or satiric episodes that often depict, in realistic detail, the everyday life of the common people' (Ilona 2005, 46, referring to the OED definition).

5   At time of writing, the translation is forthcoming: 'The Missing King', Auckland: Little Island Books, 2012. As a result, any quotations given here are non-paginated, and reference is made instead to the original *Le Roi absent* (henceforth *LRA*).

6   I have argued elsewhere that this results in a degree of didacticism over and above the usual paratextual elements (glossary, footnotes) as efforts are made to explain localisms for an out-of-country reader ('Seeing Double: Representing Otherness in the Franco-Pacific Thriller' in Anderson, J; Miranda, C; Pezzotti, B. eds. 'Representing Otherness: the Foreign in International Crime Writing', London: Continuum, 2012, 60–71).

Much has been written about the difficulty of defining humour; as Maher points out, 'we cannot help but be aware of considerable variation among individuals as to what is considered funny, and what kinds of topics it is legitimate or appropriate to laugh at' (Maher 2011, 2). However, it is generally agreed that humour can be broken down into verbal humour (such as wordplay, puns, jokes) and a more complex association (or dissociation) of contextual elements: as Antoine has put it, '*L'humour d'un texte est autant affaire de contexte, de ton, de structure, de culture, que de mots*' (Antoine 1999, 19; 'The humour of a text is just as much a matter of context, tone, structure and culture as it is of words').[7] Within the postcolonial literary context, the concept of 'laughing back', as suggested by Reichl and Stein (2005, 10), using various forms of humour such as ridicule, irony or satire, becomes a means of either lending agency or relieving tension and thereby preventing an anticipated readerly opposition; in both cases, however, its use should be seen as a deliberate authorial strategy.

While some postcolonial African writers have undertaken to 'relexify' language (Zabus 1990), this has proven to be a technique practised more by anglophone than francophone authors. There is no equivalent term in French for 'World Englishes'. As Bandia points out, 'French assimilation policy encouraged the teaching of language and literature in the colonies, whereas the British placed more emphasis on basic language skills than literature for purely expedient reasons' (Bandia 2008, 27). This, coupled with 'the attitude of French publishers who would accept nothing less than 'perfect grammar' (2008, 27), has meant that experimentation and the transfer of local structures into this particular Europhone language were relatively rare prior to Chamoiseau's 'invention' of literary *créolité* with the novel *Texaco* (1992); despite this movement, experimentation and transfer remain infrequent. Certainly within the Franco-Pacific context, linguistically non-standard (as opposed to structurally or generically non-standard) writing remains very much the exception.[8]

When creating a postcolonial text, a French-language writer, then, may be relatively cautious at the level of strictly linguistic innovation, humorous or otherwise. It is certainly the case that the challenges of translating *Le Roi absent* are not, on the whole, issues of linguistic creativity or language play, with a few important exceptions, as we shall see. The majority of the

---

7   All translations are my own.
8   The most obvious example of this exception to date would be French Polynesia's Chantal Spitz, who deliberately 'distorts' grammatical structures and transgresses genre expectations (see, for example, *Hombo* or *Elles*).

issues related to humour in this work are clustered around what I will refer to as 'incongruities', the juxtaposition of elements from different cultures or traditions in such a way as to cause a humorous effect. As Laurian and Szende have stated:

> *L'humour naît toujours d'un décalage ou d'un contraste, il y a rupture ou irruption d'un élément incongru entre signifiant et signifié, bifurcation d'un sens prévisible à un sens inattendu, suspension, voire subversion des évidences.* (Laurian and Szende 2001, 16)
>
> Humour always arises from a discrepancy or a contrast; there is a rupture or the intrusion of something incongruous between the signifier and the signified, a deviation from predictable to unpredictable meaning, a suspension or even the subversion of the expected.

I hope to show here some of the ways in which Brotherson makes use of these contrasts and unpredictable juxtapositions to question, by exploiting it in unexpected ways, the centrality of Anglo-American cultural references.

From naïve observer to cultural globalisation

Space does not permit a detailed analysis of the entire book (which is over five hundred pages long), and there are some vital twists in the plot which it seems preferable not to give away: hence I will not give a synopsis but will focus on specific aspects of the work. The first part of this can be described as an indigenous *Bildungsroman* of the 'underdog makes good despite injustice and obstacles' variety. Much of the appeal for the reader resides in Brotherson's use of humour, as we follow the adventures of an initially innocent young narrator, growing up away from home in Pape'ete and Paris, developing his considerable abilities as a chess player and pursuing his course of studies to become a civil aviation engineer. Vaki (also known, mysteriously, as Moanam)[9] is an elective mute: in other words, an indigene principally reliant on the written word for communication. The irony of this strategic choice will not escape the reader, aware that the traditional culture of French Polynesia is an oral one.

---

9   The novel opens with a reflection on Vaki's father's perplexing choice of a definitely non-Pacific name, Moana (the sea), being replaced by the strangely elongated version Moanam.

Clearly the use of an unsophisticated or uninitiated narrator is a time-honoured technique allowing for both humour and serious social criticism, the most well-known example of which in the French literary tradition is Montesquieu's *Lettres persanes* (*Persian Letters* 1721).[10] Vaki's puzzlement or naïve acceptance of people and objects (a prostitute, *steak tartare*, an escalator), encountered as a young Marquesan visiting Pape'ete for the first time, are elements which illustrate one of Brotherson's principle comedic techniques: the gap between a surface value and deeper meaning as revealed by the deadpan juxtaposition of conflicting aspects. It is worth noting here, too, his choice in the first half of the book of an apparently mildly autistic narrator-focaliser, which provides a source of humour requiring a delicate balance between an obsessive focus on detail and giftedness and an incapacity for understanding anything but surface meanings. For example, Vaki's methodical counting of paces as he walks for the first time to his Paris lodgings, his outstanding skills at chess, and his ability to solve the Rubik's cube with ease contrast with his naïve acceptance of his classmates' lies, and his inability to decipher the desperate hints of chess-club organisers that he should deliberately lose a match. While there are other examples of the kind of mitigated humour such a focus enables,[11] we might argue that in this context an allegorical reading is also possible, according to which the kinds of explorer–indigene surface interactions and subsequent misunderstandings of the 'discovery' or contact period are brought to mind, and reversed.

More concretely, Brotherson repeatedly highlights the question of cultural colonisation by frequent references to an increasingly global environment, in which contemporary media create strange bedfellows and Anglo-American 'coca-cola' influences reach to the far corners of the planet.[12] To illustrate this, we have only to look at the titles of the first two chapters of the book: from 'Mon royaume pour un cheval' ('My kingdom for a horse') we progress to 'Les cochons dans l'espace' ('Pigs in space'). There is no particular difficulty in translating these expressions, moving

---

10 One might also cite Voltaire's *L'Ingénu*, published in 1767, and featuring the visit of a young Huron to Paris in 1690, a model followed by Mordecai Richler's satirical *The Incomparable Atuk* (1963) (see Heinz 2005).

11 These traits are of course reminiscent of other works centred on autistic spectrum characters, of which the film *Rainman* (Levinson 1988) and *The Curious Incident of the Dog in the Night-Time* (Haddon 2003) are probably the best-known examples.

12 See, for example, Dunne and Tonra (1997). The term 'culture coca-cola' was a commonplace of debates in France leading to the language protection law known as the Loi Toubon, voted into effect on 4 August 2004.

from Shakespeare's *Richard III* to Jim Henson's *Muppet Show* and its parody of George Lucas's *Star Wars*.[13] Although each of these chapters puts its own spin on its title, it is worth noting the levelling out of high and low cultural references here. Brotherson has appropriated well-known cultural elements from historical as well as contemporary colonising cultures and turned them to his own purposes, making them signifiers of something other than the foreign. While this positioning side-by-side creates a comic effect, it also signals an awareness of the reach of those outside cultures into the Pacific world.

What's in a name?

A further element of humour in the novel resides in the name of the second narrator-protagonist, a psychoanalyst who is involved in Vaki's life at several crucial stages, and to whom Vaki's manuscript is later entrusted, creating a story embedded within a story, one of the layerings referred to above. This man's name is Philippe Nègre, and the chapter in which he first appears is entitled 'Philippe le nègre blanc' (Philippe the white negro). Whether this is a reference to a well-known 1968 treatise on Quebec independence, *Nègres blancs d'Amérique*, by Pierre Vallières, translated and published in 1971 as *White Niggers of America*, is unclear; if so, or if this work is known to the reader, it evokes issues of colonialism which are addressed in *Le Roi absent* only relatively indirectly. The naming of the white, French professional in this way is, however, clearly provocative. The translator is thus faced with a dilemma: should the name be translated, and if so, how? And there is more to come: in the second part of the book, Philippe receives the manuscript and tries to place it with a publisher under his own name; this is a play on words, since in French a ghost writer is called *un nègre*. Should the character's name be altered to Mr Ghost, perhaps, for the sake of the pun? Or is the semantic loading and anti-colonial humour more important to maintain? At least in the pairing of French and English it is possible to assume that Nègre will trigger the near-homophone in the target language, thus preserving some of the connotations and ironic inversions evoked in French. This is an obvious example of the kind of word play where the

---

13　Indeed, in bringing these examples into English the translator is in a way 'repatriating' the allusions. Brotherson's familiarity with Anglo-American culture may be the result of, and a comment on, the all-pervasiveness of some of its forms, but it is worth noting also that he lived and worked in New York for a number of years.

translator is obliged to choose between polysemes (Ballard 1987, 23–43). Here the overall balance of the work, with its (post)colonial context, and the fortunate existence of approximate homophony, have been judged sufficient to justify not translating the name, losing the reference to ghost-writing but preserving what was deemed to be the more important element of ironic humour.

Pseudo-code-switching: When the intralingual becomes interlingual

In aural media, a great deal of humour can be created around the issue of heavily accented pronunciation; the well-known British television series '*Allo, 'Allo!* (Croft and Lloyd 1982–1992) is an example of this.[14] A similar effect of imperfect language performance is sometimes created in literary works; here, however, the medium obviously requires different techniques, such as visibly bad grammatical structures, inappropriate vocabulary or misspellings intended to represent mispronunciations. This is not code-switching per se, which would require the speaker to bring in other languages beside the one used principally in the narrative, but a form of inter-language in which there is interference from the speaker's first language. This impacts on his or her use of the language in which the text as a whole is written, which I will refer to as the narrative language.

Translation difficulties arise when one or more characters use the narrative language in a non-standard way. These usages become even more problematic when intra-lingual imperfections (ie in the narrative language) need to be carried across into the target language, and particularly when that language is ostensibly the pseudo-code-switching character's native tongue. *Le Roi absent* features an important figure in the second half of the book, Alexander Whaler, an American whose slightly mangled French is a source of gentle humour in the original. Whaler uses the (to him) foreign language extensively; from the translator's point of view, the greater the number of utterances, and the more comment they occasion, the greater

---

14 The series was created as a parody of another BBC program, *Secret Army*, but can equally be seen as poking fun at the vast array of films with a foreign setting in which characters speak inexplicably native-accented languages from countries not their own. Linguistic veracity is a relatively recent phenomenon in the visual media, and still maintains target-audience-oriented limitations in most cases.

the challenge. Because in *Le Roi absent* Whaler comes from a long line of residents of Massachusetts, his American identity is firmly fixed in the text and integral to the plot. It is not possible to change this simply for the sake of giving him another origin, hence a reason for less than perfectly mastered English, the new narrative language (where, in the original, he used less than perfect French). Nor is it possible, I would argue, to have him speak imperfect English simply because the framing or narrative language of the text has shifted from French to English; he is after all an educated man and a well-known publisher. What is required is to create an impression of slightly mangled French, rather than text that fully reproduces every variant element. In other words, although the narrative language of the book is changed, the idea that Whaler is speaking French, not English, to his French-speaking guest, needs to be maintained. When Whaler speaks French in the original, but with a few errors, the translation needs to reflect rather than reproduce the dialogue:

> *Des Indiens? C'est normal, nous sommes ici en plein territoire Wampanoag, vous savez. Il faut je vous raconter quelque chose sur Thanksgiving. Venez, on va apporter tout ça à Earl, parce que moi, je cuisine pas!* (*LRA*, 380)

> *Des Indiens?* Not surprising, we're in Wampanoag territory here, *vous savez.* I have to tell you *quelque chose sur* Thanksgiving. We'll give all this to Earl to cook, because *moi, je cuisiner pas.*

The strategy used here has been to leave easily guessable or relatively empty French (in italics) and to introduce an error which does not in fact exist in the original (*je cuisiner pas*) to compensate for the loss of the faulty '*il faut je vous raconter*'. The English cognate borrowing, 'cuisine', should be readily understood by readers, and the relatively heavy use of French is intended to establish Whaler's preference for speaking this language; the passage is situated shortly after his first appearance in the novel. By leaving a number of French expressions here which, by and large, are guessable by anglophone readers, it is hoped that the principle of the primacy effect, that is, the early establishment of particular traits and behaviours, will mean the impression of Whaler speaking flawed French carries over through the rest of the narrative. A further typical trait in both the orginal and the translation is his frequent use of '*vous savez*', again established early and easy to maintain, since it is essentially a filler with little or no meaning other than the conative function.

Applying a similar approach, *'Non pas vraiment, j'habite ici vous savez!*
C'est ma maison' (*LRA* 383) becomes 'No, not really. I live here, *vous savez.*
C'est mon maison'; and *'Philippe, savez-vous quelle est le signification profond
de Thanksgiving?'* (*LRA* 384), with its errors of grammatical gender and
agreement, is rendered as 'Philippe, *savez-vous le signification*, the deep
meaning of Thanksgiving?', a brief gloss in English making the flawed
French accessible to any reader.

The degree to which the flaws in Whaler's French will be appreciated by
readers depends on their knowledge of that language; however, the aim of
establishing that he speaks it with both enthusiasm and a certain, mildly
amusing inaccuracy has by now been fulfilled through a minor but necessary
rewriting of the original.

Humour and the erotic

One of the most striking scenes in the novel recounts the loss of Vaki's
virginity. Having driven his fiancée to inspect progress on their soon-to-
be-completed dream home, the two move on to a lookout point, a suitably
romantic location to watch the sun set behind Moorea. Maggy, who has
previous experience, takes the initiative, and the lovemaking is recounted
from the point of view of a somewhat puzzled and semi-distracted young
man whose body escapes his control. The text sits uneasily on the border
between the description of a passionate embrace and a kind of self-mockery;
translating this comically ambiguous attitude without falling into either
purple prose or the ridiculous is no easy task:

> *Elle tourne la tête vers moi et je m'empare du lobe de son oreille. Ma langue
> est agile, la pointe durcie de ses seins me le révèle. Elle souffle, je souffle, nous
> soufflons sans parvenir à éteindre ce qui brûle nos corps. Elle se retourne et
> m'attrape la tête. Sa bouche part à l'assaut de ma langue restée dehors mais
> privée d'oreille. Comment fait-elle cela? Elle jette son sweat-shirt par-dessus
> bord et m'écrase maintenant de ses seins lourds.* (*LRA* 246)

She turns her head toward me and I move on to her earlobe. My tongue
gets busy, and her nipples harden in response. She huffs, and I puff, but
we don't blow out the fire burning up our bodies. She turns and grasps
my head. Her mouth attacks my tongue, still protruding but deprived
of her ear. How is she doing that? She throws her sweatshirt overboard
and crushes me with her heavy breasts.

The humour that seems to undercut any attempt on the reader's part to be carried away by the erotic activities arises in large part from Vaki's inability to let his senses dominate completely. The faint echo of the '*Trois petits cochons*', in which the wolf '*souffla, souffla*' to blow the house down underlines the same kind of childishness that makes him refer to his penis as his '*chose*' (thing).[15] A more adult but equally distracting comparison undermines the descriptions of fellatio and cunnilingus that follow:

> *Elle me regarde, dégage ses cheveux et reprend son apnée sensuelle. En bon mammifère elle doit bientôt reprendre son souffle avant de replonger. Le bruit de ventouse que fait sa bouche sur ma chose est indécent. Tout comme le filet de salive qui nous relie encore... Je croque la pomme, je veux connaître son secret, je veux connaître comme on connaît dans la Bible. Maggy me caresse la tête. Non, en fait elle me tire les cheveux et me plaque. Respirer... Je suis aussi un mammifère et je cherche mon souffle. (LRA 247)*

She looks into my eyes, pushes her hair out of the way, and dives back down again. A mere mammal, she'll have to surface sometime soon to breathe before the next descent. The sucking noise she makes as she lets go of my cock is obscene. As is the thread of saliva still joining us... I bite into the apple, I want to know its secret, I want to know in the biblical sense. Maggy is stroking my head. No, she's pulling my hair, planting me in position. Breathe... I'm a mammal too and I'm struggling to breathe.

Reminiscent of many an episode of awkward sexual initiation, the combination of eroticism and a distancing humour created mainly through the use of metaphoric parallels is perhaps not unlike the tone encountered in earthy eighteenth-century novels (*Fanny Hill* and *Tom Jones*, rather than *Justine* or *Juliette*). The scene closes, however, on a much darker note, despite the reassuring statement that the word modesty has no meaning '*entre deux êtres qui ne font rien de mal*' (*LRA* 248; 'between two people who aren't doing anything wrong').

---

15 While earlier in the book '*chose*' in this context was translated as 'thingy' or 'willy', terms that fitted a more childish context, here an initial translation of '*chose*' as 'thing' was rejected as sounding overly coy rather than innocent. While space does not permit a full discussion here, the translation of body parts, especially the sexual organs, is always a challenge.

The changes in tone in such quick succession, which give rise to the humour here, are very much a challenge for the translator, as the juxtaposition of conflicting impulses and values creates a scene where passion, puzzlement, humour and imaginative imagery are so very closely combined. There is also a parodic element in play, potentially evoking in the reader's mind the erotic narratives he or she may have encountered previously.[16]

Leaps of the imagination: Cultural juxtapositions

From the very first chapter, Brotherson uses a writing strategy that highlights the interchanges between Oceanian and Anglo-American cultures. 'Mon royaume pour un cheval', as we have noted, evokes Shakespearean dimensions. The chapter recounts an episode from Vaki's childhood, where he accompanied his father to hunt out a new horse. This story is anchored both in Polynesian cultural references – the people of the Marquesas islands are admired for their horsemanship – and in Hollywoodian make-believe: Vaki's father, Maheono, has worked in the film industry as a stunt-rider in Westerns, playing the parts of Indian warriors. The subtext here is clear: indigenous peoples can be substituted for one another, their cultural specificities blurred together for easier exploitation. There is a black humour also in the story of Maheono's final ride as he takes his son with him:

> Il fit une de ses cascades favorites, feignant de choir de son cheval puis me ramassa d'un geste pour me placer derrière lui. L'enlèvement de la femme blanche, je crois que c'est le nom de cette acrobatie. (*LRA* 22–23)
>
> He did one of his favourite stunts, pretending to fall off his horse, then scooped me up and put me behind him. Abducting the white woman, I think that's what that particular gymnastic feat is called.

Told from the perspective of a child, it is easy to see the impact of the Western movie on the narrator's imagination. A further example of the same influence can be found in the story of the Tahitian chess championships, where the stages of the competition become moments from *Gunfight at the OK Corral*:

---

16 I would also argue that at a more serious level the text constitutes a comment on people's propensity to self-narrate new experiences in terms of known cultural forms, ie here the actual experience is shadowed by and expressed in terms belonging to previously encountered narratives (The Three Little Pigs, the Bible, pornographic texts).

Retour dans la rue de terre rouge. L'ambiance est électrique. Frappé en plein cœur, Vetea gît face contre terre près de l'entrée du coiffeur. Maggy est assise, une balle entre les deux yeux qui continuent de clignoter dans les derniers sursauts... Je rajuste mon chapeau, souffle dans le canon de mon six-coups. Weiller, debout, regarde incrédule le trou dans sa poitrine. Il est tombé, le tueur de légende. (LRA 50–52).

Back we go into the dusty red street. The atmosphere is electric. Shot through the heart, Vetea is lying face down near the barber's doorway. Maggy is sitting there with a bullet between those eyes, still blinking, in her death throes... I tilt my hat, blow into the barrel of my six gun. Weiller just stands there, looking incredulously at the hole in his chest. The legendary killer is down.

Obviously these two passages can be read as indicators of the immense power of Hollywood's version of the Wild West to colonise our imaginations and to create a tamed and romanticised version of an earlier era when immense damage was being done to indigenous populations the world over. But we should also consider them in the context of the rest of the novel, where these ironies are underlined in a number of ways, culminating in the confusion that reigns in the mind of Vaki's former psychiatrist, Philippe Nègre, whose imagination in turn is overtaken by images and events based on Marquesan myths and history. This demonstration of the power of the indigenous story is arguably a form of 'laughing back', demonstrating the capacity of narratives from outside the Anglo-American tradition to seize our imaginations.

Concluding remarks

Even a cursory reading of theoretical works on humour translation and postcolonial translation is sufficient to make us aware that these are two areas where there is an especially sharp focus on the balance between textual features and their context of origin. In translating humorous postcolonial texts this balance is particularly important, since the comic element may well be closely related to the issues of cultures in contact and imbalances in power relations (Tymoczko and Gentzler 2002). Few translators today would think of simply proceeding joke by joke through a piece of writing, and would be aware that it is essential to reflect in some detail on the perceived function of these jokes within the larger framework of the relationship of the text to its socio-historical context. Precisely because it is not always possible to 'carry across' humour from one culture to another, and since decisions must be made repeatedly as to which aspects to lose and which to attempt at all costs to maintain, the translator must be prepared to consider each of these decisions at both macro- and micro-structural levels. Recognising that Brotherson's *Le Roi absent* asserts the power of French Polynesian culture to appropriate other, 'global' cultural forms is an important factor in determining how to manage the process of humour translation throughout the book. In addition to the dominance of the Marquesan imaginary over the trained mind of the Frenchman Philippe Nègre,[17] whose name takes on another level of significance as a result of this subjugation, there is an episode much earlier in the book that I consider key to understanding the dynamics of *Le Roi absent*, of which humour is a strong element. This episode contains the image of Tahitian students in Paris transferring their sense of belonging from the South Seas to the Place de la Sorbonne, in a kind of rebirth, a moment of apparently little importance in Vaki's life and in the novel:

> *J'eus un instant l'étrange vision de cérémonies secrètes où... les étudiants sortis du 62 rue Monsieur le Prince, venaient tour à tour soulever un des deux mille huit cent soixante-sept pavés de la place, pour y déposer religieusement son placenta ultra-marin.* (*LRA* 174)

> For a moment I had a strange vision of secret ceremonies in which the students from 62 Rue Monsieur le Prince... stepped forward in turn to lift up one of the two thousand eight hundred and sixty-seven cobblestones in the Place, and reverently place beneath them their placentas from over the seas.

This ambiguous image can be read two ways: either the Tahitian students are becoming French, tied to the land by their placentas – an assimilationist view of the colonisation of French Polynesia – or on the contrary, they are claiming France and Paris as their own, creating a link between their birthplace (and birthright) and '*le centre du monde culturel*' (*LRA* 165, 'the centre of the cultural world'). I believe that this scene underlines one of *Le Roi absent*'s key messages: colonised peoples are capable of taking their place within and alongside so-called dominant cultures, of testing the strength of

---

17 It should also be noted that despite the historic links between French Polynesia and France, there are far fewer references to French cultural elements than to Anglo-American ones. This is in itself perhaps a rejection of colonial power relations.

their own cultures against these, and indeed of appropriating them for their own purposes and bending them around their own lives and narratives just as this novel does.

References

Antoine, Fabrice; Wood, Mary, eds. 1999. *Humour, culture, tradition(s)*. Ateliers, 19. Cahiers de la maison de recherche Elextra. Lille: Université Charles de Gaulle.

Bandia, Paul F. 2008. *Translation as Reparation: Writing and Translation in Postcolonial Africa*. Manchester: St. Jerome.

Brotherson, Moetai. 2007. *Le Roi absent*. Pape'ete: Au vent des îles.

Chamoiseau, Patrick. 1992. *Texaco*. Paris: Gallimard.

Chiaro, Delia, ed. 2010. *Translation, Humour and the Media*. Translation and Humour, Vol. 2. Continuum Advances in Translation. London: Continuum.

Croft, David; Lloyd, Jeremy. 1982–1992. *'Allo, 'Allo!* BBC One.

Dunne, Denise; Tonra, Ben. 1997. 'A European cultural identity – myth, reality or aspiration.' Occasional paper. Dublin: The Institute of European Affairs, Dublin. Accessed 27 October 2011. Available from: http://ucd-ie.academia.edu/BenTonra/ Papers/325280/The_European_Cultural_Identity_Myth_Reality_or_Aspiration.

Haddon, Mark. 2003. *The Curious Incident of the Dog in the Night-time*. London: Doubleday.

Heinz, Anton. 2005. 'Postcolonial laughter in Canada'. In *Cheeky Fictions: Laughter and the Postcolonial*, edited by Reichl, Susanne; Stein, Mark. Amsterdam: Rodopi: 89–106.

Henson, Jim. 1976–1981. *The Muppet Show*. ITC Entertainment/Henson Associates.

Ilona, Anthony. 2005. 'Laughing through the tears. In *Cheeky Fictions: Laughter and the Postcolonial*, edited by Reichl, Susanne; Stein, Mark. Amsterdam: Rodopi: 43–60.

Laurian, Anne-Marie; Szende, Thomas Szende, eds. 2001. *Les Mots du rire: comment les traduire? Essais de lexicologie contrastive*. Bern: Peter Lang.

Levinson, Barry, dir. 1988. *Rainman*. MGM.

Lucas, George, dir. 1977. *Star Wars*. 20th Century Fox.

Maher, Brigid. 2011. *Recreation and Style: Translating Humorous Literature in Italian and English*. Amsterdam: John Benjamins.

Reichl, Susanne; Stein, Mark, eds. 2005. *Cheeky Fictions: Laughter and the Postcolonial*. Rodopi, Amsterdam.

Shakespeare, William. (c. 1591) *Richard III*.

Spitz, Chantal. 2002. *Hombo*. Pape'ete: Editions Te Iti.

Spitz, Chantal. 2011. *Elles*. Pape'ete: Au Vent des îles.

Tymoczko, Maria; Gentzler, Edwin, eds. 2002. *Translation and Power*. Amherst: University of Massachusetts Press.

Tymoczko, Maria. 1999. *Translation in a Postcolonial Context: Early Irish Literature in English Translation*. Manchester: St Jerome.

Chapter 8

Toil, trouble and *jouissance*

A case study – editing *Juan the Landless*

Peter Bush

Narrating the storyline of a literary translation might be the most appropriate way of approaching a translator's description of how it was written. It seems a straightforward enough notion – the pursuit of a linear sequence of steps that connect a novel written in one language, by a dead or living author, to the version that a publisher (in a particular country, or a transnational conglomerate), commissions and contracts a translator to transform into another language to a deadline. The submission of a virtual manuscript sets in motion an editing process which climaxes in final packaging, publication and promotion, the appearance of a book in shops and online market places, and the eventual reactions of readers and critics. All this activity takes place in a particular historical context and is the hub for a complex interplay between individuals that, primed with their different subjectivities, personal agendas and cultural politics, intervene in the creation of the translation. Familiar to all professional translators, the stark time line should be the necessary starting point for a discussion of creative constraints in literary translation. The interplay is there to be analysed on the basis of empirical evidence – the archives of writers, publishers and translators – underpinned by a critical perspective that encompasses everything from biography to the economy. The overarching impulse would surely be the illumination, through case studies, of an art that is a unique form of writing central to the very existence of human culture. Such studies would, then, be central to the education of literary translators.

The workshop experience

Conversely, although the above is present implicitly in the act of translating, the momentum of that act is driven by the desire to create an 'excellent' translation. When we sat around a table in the Wheeler Centre translating Jorge Carrión's text during the Monash *Translated!* workshop, we read, re-read, drafted and re-drafted our individual translations, though the focus was on the final collaboratively translated version. The context was a translation workshop that I led with ten or so translators. We did not simply want to finish up with ten different versions: Jorge and I had made it plain that we wanted the end product to be published – as it duly was. So, the simulation was more than an exercise. Many participants brought to the seminar draft translations that were quite advanced, so the final translation was the fruit of more than a week's exposure to the text. Jorge was there at the beginning to introduce his novel and the thinking behind it, and also at intervals during the week to answer questions and comment on interpretations and solutions. The tutor-translator doubled as publisher's editor: I did a final edit on the English translation that was eventually published as a result of contact the novelist had made with a literary website in the USA.

Our discussions were interpretive and considered the media sources of the narrative and its registers, as well as the parallel rhythm and registers in English. With this text, the translation was helped by the fact that many of the sources were American television series; it was in itself a collage of translations. Even so, the final version was the result of intense debate and re-writing, but at no stage did any participant give up on the collaboration and make an appeal to total relativity. There were very active cursors in operation and they responded to degrees of literary quality in the writing: it seemed possible to affirm this word or sentence was better than that. Unlike the academic translations-studies analysis that is concerned with finding what is interesting from theoretical perspectives in sets of translations of the same text, a translation workshop, posited on publication, is guided by the need for a single excellent outcome in practice, and in that sense recognises the supremacy of practice. We translate to be read, not to be analysed or theorised. Literary translation is, after all, a branch of literature, not an extension of literary theory or criticism. It is also worth emphasising that all participants had a high level of competence in both English and Spanish, which meant the various edits and hundreds of decisions were informed by that knowledge. No editor-translator there was blindly groping for 'good literary English' in the abstract with no sense at all of the original.

The publishing history of *Juan the Landless*

When I left the British Centre for Literary Translation and went to live in Barcelona, I decided to return to the London Book Fair every year to maintain a minimum visibility with publishers and attend translation events that were becoming more and more common. During a couple of these visits I spoke to Chad Post, then at the Dalkey Archive Press, who was enthusiastic about the possibility of retranslating the trilogy that marked Spanish novelist Juan Goytisolo's break with linear narrative and critical realism, and his launch into more adventurous, modernist fiction: *Señas de identidad* (1966), *Reivindicación del conde Julián* (1970) and *Juan sin tierra* (1975). These had been translated into English and first published by Viking Penguin in the USA, and then re-issued by Seaver Books in New York and Serpent's Tail in the UK: *Marks of Identity* by Gregory Rabassa, *Count Julian* and *Juan the Landless* (1977 and 1990) by Helen Lane. Given that the rights of the previous publishers had expired, it was now possible to re-translate, and it would make sense to have the trilogy translated by a single translator; by this time I had translated a number of Juan Goytisolo's fictions, including *Quarantine*. Dalkey is mainly dedicated to bringing modernist literature into English, and is developing a considerable list of contemporary Hispanic literature, so the idea proved appealing to them. I had hoped to have an opportunity to retranslate the trilogy, particularly because Juan Goytisolo had recently revised the texts for publication by Galaxia Gutenberg in Barcelona in what he ironically refers to as his 'Incomplete Works', given that he is still alive and writing. Yet Dalkey succeeded in securing rights to publish translations of only the first two novels in the trilogy, so I was thwarted in that regard and left with the challenge of *Juan the Landless*, which the author had revised by cutting over forty per cent of the text. He was insisting on a new translation, even though a cut-and-paste job on Helen Lane's translation would have been feasible, if inappropriate, because her brilliant translation worked with the meandering, expansive nature of the first original; Goytisolo's surgery had thrown the remains into completely different relief. In the meantime, Chad Post had departed to set up a new translation press and centre in Rochester.

Editors, translators and final edits: Behind the scenes

Often one of the unknowns for a translator is the publisher's eventual strategy for the editing of the translation. I have written about issues that arose in Dalkey's edit of *Quarantine* in the *Times Literary Supplement* (Bush 1996).

The editor claimed I was making Goytisolo more difficult than he was in the original and that by using words such as 'knacker's yard' and 'gentles' (being UK English or even, according to the *Oxford English Dictionary*, archaic UK English), my translation would not be understood by 'the man in the street'. I pointed out that this mythical man was unlikely, unfortunately, to be buying Dalkey and reading Juan Goytisolo, and so my Shakespearian English finally passed muster – but not before offering another instance of an apparently plausible editorial criterion that in the end was simply superficial.

A few months before embarking on *Juan the Landless*, Dalkey Archive had also asked me to act as an arbitrator in a dispute they were having with a translator. I duly read a chapter or so of the original text, the original translation and the Dalkey edit. My report indicated weaknesses in the original translation – I felt it required a few more drafts, a little more time for reflection and rewriting, but that it was on the right track – and concluded that the edit was taking the translation into a more conventional mode. In other words, the translator was attempting to be equally adventurous as the original writer, and the edit was curbing the spirit of adventure in favour of conventionality, albeit of a highbrow variety. In the end, the translator's final translation was severely edited and published on the basis of the ultimatum: Accept the edit, or your translation will never be published. Clearly, contractually publishers have the last word.

The incident reveals how fraught the editing of literary translations can sometimes be and illustrates what the translator must be prepared to handle. This is not a level of conflict that is only faced by relatively new translators. When I visited Helen Lane in Albuquerque, she told me that she was on the point of taking her publisher to court for changes they had introduced into a translation she had done of work by a leading Latin-American novelist. On another occasion, I invited Edith Grossman to lead a workshop in the BCLT Literary Translation Summer School and she refused point-blank to come to a session with a publisher I had invited to speak on the topic of publishing translations. Why? Because of the way that publisher had edited her American-English translations, again, of leading Latin-American writers. I think these eruptions reveal the level of emotional and intellectual commitment by translators to their work. It doesn't mean they (or their editors) are necessarily always 'right', nor do such eruptions take place with every book, but they should be borne in mind by those involved in educating literary translators and those evaluating translations without access to drafts and edits. To put these comments into perspective, I have translated over sixty works and have only twice experienced serious conflict over a translation with a publisher.

In the meantime, Katherine Silver, a friend, experienced translator and now co-director of the Banff Centre, alerted me to a dialogue in Dalkey's online journal *Context* in which the publishing director, John O'Brien, and one of his main editors, Jeremy Davies, give 'practical information about what goes on behind the scenes at Dalkey' and 'by extension the world of literary translation publishing in general' (O'Brien and Davies 2011, 1). (This 'world' refers, of course, to the very sui generis English-speaking world of the infamous Three Percent publishing output of translations and of the predominantly monolingual editor.)

The main tenor of the *Context* dialogue is that translators tend to stay too close to the original, and are not explicit enough for the 'poor monophone, but intelligent and fiction-savvy reader' as Davies describes, presumably, the standard Dalkey customer, or even, perhaps, himself. Indeed, 'they have no business submitting a single sentence that they themselves cannot explain and unpick'. When I first read this, I baulked a little at the tone: it seemed to echo so many arguments I have had with those who believe that literary translation is about meaning, or those who confuse critical discussion of literature with the act of translation. It is one thing – and no mean thing! – to be able to 'unpick' Mallarmé's 'L'après-midi d'un faune' or Joyce's *Ulysses*, quite another to translate them, and the difference is the chasm between analytical criticism and literary creation. The relative articulacy of literary translators about what they have done is absolutely no indication of the quality of their translations, one way or the other. In the *Context* dialogue, there is praise quite rightly for Barbara Wright, the great translator of Queneau, Sarraute and others. Wright had enormous ability in approaching the originals and recreating them in English, but almost none when it came to attempting to explain what she had done. In retrospect, I should have realised the ominous nature of Davies's remarks.

Davies was to edit my translation of Goytisolo's *Juan the Landless* and on almost every page of his edit he requested that I explain some cultural, historical or political reference. I finally decided that my only response could be that it was not my role to explain to him or to future readers any of this. I had done the online or library research where necessary, or relied on my own knowledge, or asked the author, in that time-consuming scholarly activity that all translators must engage in. Why had I done this? In the expectation that information would help in the creation of the literary text I was writing. That writing, like Goytisolo's, would have to stand – or fall – by itself. The reader could take it from there. The literary translator can produce a critical edition with scholarly apparatus, if that is required, for university students, but not a 'shadow' one for the benefit of editors.

Original readers and great writers

John O'Brien continues the dialogue with two ideas that are frequently rehearsed in exchanges on literary translation and seem to me to belong to an immediately appealing, again superficially plausible, but at the same time critically flawed set of prescriptions. The first is that the translator's goal must be to recreate the experience of the 'original readers'. Does one track the latter down, questionnaire at the ready? '*Señora, señor,* what was it like for you reading Juan Goytisolo's trilogy during the decline of the Generalísimo's dictatorship?' Were these readers in Madrid, Bilbao, Sevilla or Barcelona? Or were they indeed exiled like Goytisolo himself in Paris, or else in Mexico City or Lima or Havana? Or what if they were fascists? And thirty years later, what will they remember of what undeniably must have been a riotously disturbing and severely demanding, and even possibly clandestine, read? Of course, we could ask Spanish readers today but they could not be categorised as 'original' readers. We might at most ascertain memories of general impressions, responses to certain passages, perhaps. But perhaps I also qualify as an original reader: I read the books when they were first published in Spanish! My reactions belong to the immediate reader as translator as well as the historically formed imagination of someone who has lived in and out of Spain during the dictatorship, transition to democracy and now in Barcelona for the past eight years.

The second idea is that 'the best translators are great poets and writers', the implication being that 'just' translators are somehow automatically inferior. Again, it might sound plausible to the lay reader but what about the difficulty that many writers – in the English-speaking world, that is – have with their lack of knowledge of languages (meaning that they must rely on a crib provided by a real translator)? Also, what about the temptation that writers often feel to adapt the style of the translation to their own literary style? It might read well but might have become disconnected from the original, not that the 'monophone' editor would notice. And these so-called versions are surely a long way from that experience of the original readers.

An academic parenthesis: Literary translation and universities

In the second part of their conversation, Davies and O'Brien decry the lack of recognition given to literary translation in the academy; they recognise that it is an art that does depend on scholarship, and that it is ridiculous for university research-assessment exercises to award points to articles about the novels of Thomas Bernhardt and none to translations that make these works available in English. It is unfortunate that the first part of their dialogue does not get beyond the commonplace and focus on artistic creativity. The way to give translation university validation is to establish literary translation in parallel to creative writing. It is not 'just' a question of editing or else we might also be forced to argue that the best editors would be great poets and writers. We then confront another irony of the situation in the English-speaking world: most professors of translation studies are linguists, historians or literary critics. Nobody would appoint a professor of creative writing who was not an established writer, poet or dramatist, yet job descriptions for professors of translation studies routinely make no mention of the need for any substantial experience of translating. Academics with such experience tend to be found in comparative or English literature or in modern languages. Clearly there is no reason why professors of translation studies should be translators, just as professors of literature do not need to be novelists or poets. The imbalance exists in translation because, while translation studies has grown, there has been no equivalent growth in what we might call the professional practice of translation as a university discipline parallel to creative writing, with staff who have had substantial professional experience.

My university experience in the UK is instructive in terms of the difficulty of establishing literary translation as a valid research practice. I was professor of literary translation at the University of Middlesex and the University of East Anglia at times that coincided with the first and second UK Research Assessment Exercises (RAE). (The fact that two universities should have a professor of literary translation was in itself a small step forward – I had requested that title as opposed to professor of translation studies.) In the first round of the RAE, Middlesex University put forward four translations as my four key publications, as part of the submission from the school of modern languages. My translations received no points. At a subsequent 'feedback' session for staff of the school, the professor of Spanish who had presided over the RAE panel began his report by saying that however excellent my translations might be – and here he mentioned one in particular, *The Marx Family Saga* by Juan Goytisolo – from the point of view of a research exercise, they might as well go into the wastepaper bin. At around the same time, the Instituto Cervantes initiated the award of the Valle-Inclán Literary Translation Prize and, with the UK Society of Authors, set up to decide the award a committee headed by that very same professor of Spanish. His committee awarded the prize to my translation of *The Marx Family Saga*! The apparent contradiction illustrates how deep the opposition is to academic acceptance of scholarship embedded in the creativity of translations. This professor's reactions are symptomatic of an ideological stance, not of any personal prejudice. In fact, the RAE language panels and European studies panel were all negative towards translations and writing in the respective languages they were assessing. The German panel, for example, awarded W. G. Sebald no recognition for his novels that had been submitted from the University of East Anglia's School of Languages. I was in good company in being pointless.

When it came to the second RAE five years later, I was one of Sebald's colleagues at the University of East Anglia. I had taken the British Centre of Literary Translation (BCLT) from the school of European languages into the school of English literature and creative writing. W. G. Sebald was by now an internationally acclaimed novelist and had also moved into creative writing. The UEA strategy was now to include my translations and Sebald's German novels in English translation by Anthea Bell and Michael Hulse as part of the submission from creative writing alongside the poetry of Andrew Motion and novels, autobiography and drama by other professors of creative writing. The UEA presented this move as a great innovation in the field of creative writing. The strategy, spearheaded by two professors of English literature, Jon Cook and the late Lorna Sage, was successful and the submission was given a very high rating. A spin-off from the progress in research recognition was the greater number of literary translations on reading lists for students of English literature and creative writing. Another key element in the creative writing–translating melting pot was the retranslation of French poetry and associated theorising by Clive Scott, professor of French literature, who had also shifted schools.

A writer's self-edit and implications for retranslation

I worked over two years from first draft to final edit on *Juan the Landless*. I became very familiar with the two originals but not their English translations. I prefer to look at existing translations when I feel my own is almost at a publishable stage. In the introduction to the Galaxia Gutenberg volume Juan Goytisolo explains why he made such a large number of changes. He removed sections that were ironic celebrations of different parts of the Islamic world – now printed separately as a miscellany of travel texts at the end of that volume – and sequences that were parodies of a professor of linguistics who was a contemporary of his at New York University – 'heavy stodge the reader can well do without' (Goytisolo 2006b, 23). Otherwise, there was no stylistic refashioning. The honing was to allow the violence of the 'hymn to Evil' and surrealist 'destructive poetic rage' to ride supreme in the attack on Spanish imperialism, its ideology, global bourgeois conventions, and suppression of the sensual, the sexual and the anal; it is a turbulent narrative punctuated by reflections on the phallic art of writing. The long and short excisions, for the sake of consistency, create a completely different ambience and rhythm even though the words that survived the cull are the same as in the first version. The abridged text boasts a sharper focus, a more intense beat, a more frenetic pace, a necklace of savage satires that bring to the fore the joyfully vicious onslaught on the standard language of polite society and conformist literary prose. Goytisolo's literary dynamiting of pomp, platitude and exploitation explodes in its purest form, as he asserts in his prologue: 'I know of no other book in peninsular Spanish literature that has these features' (Goytisolo 2006b, 24).

My desire to translate Juan Goytisolo and this particular text is clearly based on a sympathy for the politics of his art. It gives me the opportunity as translator to perform a similar attack on conventional English literary language and introduce into the English-reading world a satire that is in some cases specifically Hispanic – the Church, the Inquisition, the reclaiming of the Hispano-Arabic tradition – and in others resonates against the values of the neo-liberal world – the enthroning of the Pro Nuptia Couple, or the commercially marketed, idealised newlyweds; the obfuscation of elemental, necessary human activities that produce sex and shit; the oppression of linguistic difference…

Finally, the challenge to the literary translator is artistic: Can you write like Juan Goytisolo in English? Can you, the would-be translator of Cervantes, write like Cervantes? Can you, the would-be translator of Joyce, write like Joyce? Apart from understanding, intuiting, researching and interpreting the text in a succession of rereadings, can you also recreate that rhetoric in your own language? These are not theoretical questions: they spring from the unique dialectic of reading and writing in the art of literary translation. Nor is this *belle-lettriste*: to be able to contemplate such translations assumes a high level of scholarship, critical consciousness, a sophisticated individual history of reading, writing and living in the two languages involved, and the ability to engage and collaborate with writers and editors.

The pleasures of recreation

After the toil and trouble of my title, we now reach the pleasuring, the *jouissance*: literary translation is about the playful relishing of language in the creation of a new literary text. I will now consider three short excerpts related to *Juan the Landless* that can illuminate the playfulness, the intuitive leaps and imaginative lexical adventures without which the complexity of the translation process and its scholarly and critical dimensions would never shape into a work of art. Included are excerpts from the two original versions (JG1 and JG2; Goytisolo 1975 and Goytisolo 2006a), from Helen Lane's translation (HL; Goytisolo 1977), from my second draft and advanced uncorrected galley (PB1 and PB2; Goytisolo 2009c and 2009a), and from my editor at Dalkey (JD; Goytisolo 2009c).

i)

: *pasmada aún por el volatinero virtuosismo de la ya defunta Paloma : pero*
(JG1, 56)

pasmada aún por el volatinero virtuosismo de la ya defunta Paloma pero
(JG2, 631)

she is still stunned by the acrobatic virtuosity of the now-deceased Dove : (HL, 44)

still stunned by the recently deceased Pigeon's fleeting virtuosity but (PB1, 40)

still stunned by the deceased Pigeon's fleeting virtuosity on the wing but (PB2, 41)

Goytisolo's text has no conventional sentences and is punctuated by colons. Here we see how the author has axed some colons in his revision. Lane or her editors have turned the translation into a conventional sentence. I focused on the sound and the rhythm – the echoing sounds and the poetic balance of the two halves of the phrase. I subsumed the '*ya*' or 'now' into the 'fleeting'. The translation of '*paloma*' is always vexed, given that it can mean 'pigeon' or 'dove' and that practically and symbolically the dove has come to be the gentle symbol of peace while the pigeon is the dirty scavenger. This line comes from a highly surreal version of the Annunciation when the bird–Holy Spirit rapes the black mother Leda-like and at one point in the act transmutes into the son of the slave-owning plantation owner. The bird is not merely bringing the glad tidings. It is copulating. The situation seems to call for 'pigeon', or so I felt. I was also re-reading *Ulysses* as one way of priming my literary language and was delighted to come across a sequence where the Holy Spirit is referred to as a pigeon. Here, my editor wanted to know: 'why not dove?' and insistently highlighted every mention of the bird in yellow as if signalling the need to change. I explained how pigeon-fancying was a popular pastime in Spain and how the Federation was highly supportive of the Francoist dictatorship, underlining the negative, and hence the earthier, grittier pigeon rather than the traditionally dovish qualities of this particularly aggressive '*paloma*'.

ii)

sí, mi negra, sí, soy yo, tu Palomica, el mejor de los Tres, el santo patrono de la Federación Colombófila : (JG1, 57; JG2, 631)

yes, my black beauty, yes, it is I, your Turtledove, the best of the Three, the blessed patron of the Dove Breeders Association : (HL, 45)

yes, my black beauty, yes, it's me, your lickle Pigeon, the best of the Three, the holy patron of the Pigeon-Owners Federation : (PB1, 41)

yes, my black beauty, yes, it's me, your lickle Pigeon, the best of the Trio, the Pigeon Fanciers' Federation's holy patron : (PB2, 42)

Both HL and I use 'black beauty', not a surprising coincidence, given the political and literary connotations of the two words: certain conjunctures can coax out similar responses. The diminutive '*palomica*' is a typical diminutive from south-east Spain and Cuba. I have made three choices over these drafts that bring to the Pigeon's talk a touch of extreme, perhaps idiotic, childishness: 'lickle'; a hint of offensive familiarity to the description of the Holy Trinity, 'the Trio'; and, rounding this off, the fully proletarian notion of the 'pigeon fancier', which, in the context, plays with the obscenity of the rape, turning it back to front, as it were, in the suggestion that a pigeon fancier is one who fancies pigeons.

iii)

libradas de sus mazmorras y grillos, las palabras al fin, las traidoras, esquivas palabras, vibren, dancen, copulen, se encueren y cobren cuerpo (JG1, 218; JG2, 696)

> at last words freed from their dungeons and chains, treacherous, elusive words, vibrate, dance, copulate, strip naked, and assume carnal form (HL, 193)

> released from their dungeons and chains, words at last, treacherous, evasive words, vibrate, dance, copulate, strip off and flesh out (PB1,113)

> released from their chains and dungeons, words, treacherous elusive words, at last quiver dance copulate strip off and flesh out (PB2, 119)

> released from their chains, their dungeons, those words, those treacherous elusive words, quiver at last and dance and copulate, removing their rags and clothing themselves in flesh (JD, 130)

One of the themes of Goytisolo's text is the act of writing, and a number of chapters act as commentaries on his refashioning of language. As I have already mentioned, the impact of the writer's self-edit is to sharpen the remaining language, making the same words appear more incisive and in this case pinpointing that very process: the fresh edit has been a second release. Lane's translation ends with a juxtaposition of two different registers: 'strip naked', which is direct and vaguely sensationalist, and 'assume carnal form', which has biblical echoes of words made flesh, a move entirely in the spirit of the first version. My translation aims for spareness and verbal rhythm – hence the use of 'elusive' rather than 'evasive', 'quiver' rather than 'vibrate', and the dramatic contrast of 'strip off' and 'flesh out', with the final two words suggesting both nakedness and words that are fleshed out paradoxically by their nakedness. Explanation makes it all sound very rational, but the rush of words came with the apparent spontaneity of the writing of the translation. The words undergo two changes through self-edit, and the removal of the final commas was an excellent suggestion from Katherine Silver because it intensifies the baring of the words. Davies's edit brought in a wordy language that may have been in that spirit of making things clearer as mentioned in the *Context* conversation, but was completely at odds with the aesthetic of my translation and the author's revision, like the majority of Davies's edits, and so I rejected it as I did most of the others.

In conclusion, the experience of the Monash workshop signalled the possibility of harmonious collaboration in the process of literary translation. In that sense, it built on the approach of the BCLT International Summer School that I established when I was its director. The Monash workshop was exhilarating because of the high level of the participants, who all had an excellent knowledge of both Spanish and English, and sensitive literary responses. In this chapter, I have examined the complexity and sensitivities involved in translating for publication, and how those interactions, as recorded in drafts, edits and parallel translations, might relate to the education of literary translators. I chose an example that might be seen as polemical because it would be wrong to think that harmony always rules – strife has its creative side in an interpretive art – and that involves a press that is pioneering in its publications and in the university role it plays. The more behind-the-scenes case studies of literary translations we have, the more they can illuminate the complexities of the process, and make descriptions more accurate and less dependent on over-simplistic metaphors or analogies.

References

Bush, Peter. 1996. 'It doesn't sound like English'. *Times Literary Supplement* 4875: 11.

Goytisolo, Juan. 1975. *Juan sin tierra*. Barcelona: Seix Barral.

Goytisolo, Juan. 2006a. *Juan sin tierra*. In *Obras completas III, Juan Goytisolo novelas (1966-1982)*. Barcelona: Galaxia Gutenberg Círculo de Lectores, 595–724.

Goytisolo, Juan. 2006b. 'Prologue'. In *Obras completas III, Juan Goytisolo novelas (1966-1982)*. Barcelona: Galaxia Gutenberg Círculo de Lectores, 22–29.

Goytisolo, Juan. 1977. *Juan the Landless*. Trans. Lane, Helen R. New York: Viking Penguin; London: Serpent's Tail.

Goytisolo, Juan. 2009a. *Juan the Landless*. Trans. Bush, Peter. Champaign, Illinois: Dalkey Archive Press.

Goytisolo, Juan. 2009b. 'Afterword'. In *Juan the Landless*, translated by Peter Bush, Champaign, Illinois: Dalkey Archive Press: 155–163.

Goytisolo, Juan. 2009c. Juan the Landless, drafts, translator's own archive, which is in the course of being lodged in the Lilly Research Library, University of Indiana at Bloomington.

O'Brien, John; Davies, Jeremy N. 'Translation editing: An unedited conversation'. *Context* 22. Accessed 15 November 2011. Available from:http://www.dalkeyarchive.com/reviews/context/.

Part III

Translations

Chapter 9

The cemetery at sea

Written by Jorge Carrión

Translated by Joel Calizaya, Ana Cano Gomez, Hanna Lofgren, Adriana Rozada,
Kay Rozynski, Jarrah Strunin, Kieran Tapsell and Imogen Williams

Led by Peter Bush

'El cementerio marino' is a chapter from Jorge Carrión's *Los muertos* (Barcelona: Mondadori, 2011). The novel is a pastiche divided into two parts: the first imitates a US TV series, while the second is composed of two academic articles that analyse the social effects that this imaginary series is causing among its millions of viewers. While slight, *Los muertos* is thematically rich, traversing such territory as intellectual property, death and memory. Its focus on how to talk about horror, war and violence today positions it within post-Sebaldian catastrophe literature.

El cementerio marino

«¿Cuántas horas te has pasado aquí tumbado, cariño?», le pregunta Selena, mientras le acaricia el pelo. «Todo el día… He estado pensando, no voy a buscar mi comunidad, quiero decir que ya tengo una comunidad, no necesito la otra, aunque la otra sea la auténtica…», dice Lenny con voz de resaca. «Nada es auténtico, papá.» «Tienes razón, cielo, tienes toda la razón del mundo, pero sí hay algo real: vosotras dos sois mi comunidad.» Una cadena de manos como eslabones. «Precisamente yo venía a deciros que…», empieza a decir Jessica. Los padres enfocan con atención el rostro de la joven «…que he encontrado mi comunidad. Habréis oído hablar de ella, se llama la Comunidad de la Estrella. Desde niña sabía que había estado en una especie de gueto, desde niña los adivinos me han hablado de cuánta muerte contemplé antes de materializarme; pero hasta ahora no había encontrado el camino, quiero decir que hasta ahora no había sentido la necesidad de pertenecer… de pertenecer a una unidad superior, ¿sabéis?, a algo más grande que nosotros, o que Samuel y yo. Es una comunidad poderosa. La mayoría comparte el recuerdo de haber sido marcada, estigmatizada, con dos triángulos superpuestos. Voy a afiliarme.» «Es curioso», tercia Selena, «cómo pasan los años entre conversaciones superficiales; importantes, porque expresan cariño, pero superficiales, al fin y al cabo, y sólo a veces, diez o doce veces en toda una vida, hablamos de lo que realmente importa.» Roy y Selena se miran. «Tienes razón, Selena, por eso ha llegado el momento de hablarle de Nadia.»

Richie Aprile es despertado con violencia. Una brigada municipal, integrada por tres gigantes con uniformes blancos oficiales lo cogen en volandas para conducirlo al furgón también blanco que hay aparcado a unos cinco metros de donde el Nuevo dormía. Por sorpresa, Richie Aprile se desembaraza de sus captores y sale corriendo. Ellos no se inmutan. Una vez haya desaparecido de su vista, la respiración sacudida por la carrera, se sentará en el suelo y presionará sus sienes con los dedos índice y corazón de cada mano. «Piensa, joder, piensa.» Está temblando. Duda. Titubea. Al fin, actúa. Tras rebuscar en todos sus bolsillos, reúne unos sesenta dólares entre billetes y monedas. Ordena los billetes y los dobla; junta todo el dinero en un único bolsillo. Se ha serenado. Se peina con los dedos. Se incorpora. Comienza a caminar, buscando con la mirada, entre los locales que pueblan la avenida siguiente, alguno en cuya fachada pueda leerse: «Internet». Lo encuentra. Una decena de adolescentes juegan en otras tantas computadoras. En el mostrador del fondo le pregunta al encargado: «¿Cuánto cuesta?». «Tres dólares la hora.» «¿Y si tú me ayudas?» El encargado le responde contrariado: «Diez pavos más, tío». «Que sean siete.» «Hecho. ¿Eres nuevo, verdad?» «Más o menos.» «Venga, suelta qué estás buscando.»

The cemetery at sea

'How long have you been lying here, honey?' asks Selena, stroking his hair. 'All day... I've been thinking, I'm not going to look for my community,' says Lenny, hung-over. 'I mean I already have a community, I don't need the other one, even if it is for real...' 'Nothing is real, Dad.' 'You're right, sweetie, you're absolutely right, but there is one thing that's real: you two are my community.' A chain of hands... 'Actually, I came here precisely to tell you...' Jessica begins. The girl's parents focus intently on her face. '...that I've found my community. You've probably heard of it: the Community of the Star. As a child I knew that I had been in a kind of ghetto. Since childhood the oracles have spoken to me about all that death I witnessed before I materialized. But until now I hadn't found the path; I mean, until now I'd never felt the need to belong... to belong to a superior entity, you know? To something bigger than us, or than Samuel and me. It's a powerful community. Most of them share the same memory of being marked, stigmatized, with two triangles, one above the other. I'm going to join.' 'It's curious,' interrupts Selena, 'how the years go by in superficial conversations, important enough because they express affection, but superficial, in the end, because rarely, only eight or nine times in a lifetime, do we talk about what really matters.' 'You're right Selena.' Roy and Selena look at each other. 'Which is why it's time to tell her about Nadia.'

Richie Aprile gets a violent awakening. A municipal unit, three huge men in white uniform, haul him off the ground and carry him to the van that's also white and parked about five yards from where the New One was sleeping. Richie Aprile suddenly breaks free and runs for it. The men don't move. Out of sight, breathless from running, he sits on the ground and presses his fingers to his temples. Think, shit, think. He's shaking. He doubts, hesitates. Then acts. Rummaging through his pockets he scrapes together sixty dollars out of bills and loose change. He smoothes out the bills, folds them around the coins, and puts the money into one pocket. He's calmed down. He flattens his hair. He stands up. He starts walking, searching the shop-fronts down the next avenue for an Internet sign. He spots one. A bunch of teenagers are playing on the computers. 'How much?' he asks the guy at the desk at the back. 'Three bucks an hour.' 'And if you give me a hand?' Annoyed, the guy rasps, 'Ten bucks extra, man.' 'Seven.' 'OK, deal.' 'You're a New One, yeah?' 'Kind of.' 'So what're you after?'

Gutiérrez siente el tacto blando del cemento en sus pies. Está de pie, dentro de un recipiente de un metro cúbico exacto, con el cañón de una pistola posado en el ojo derecho. «No morirías, pero sería muy, pero que muy doloroso… Hay quien recuerda que en la otra vida a este tipo de muerte se le llamaba "Moe Green Special"», le dice el pistolero. «Michael, no entiendo por qué…» «¡Señor Corleone! ¡Te he dicho mil veces que has perdido el derecho a llamarme por mi nombre de pila, chivato de mierda!» En derredor de ambos y del recipiente lleno de cemento, cinco hombres trajeados actúan de espectadores o de coro mudo. «No quiero ir al cementerio, por Dios, no quiero estar allí con todos los que yo mismo enterré, no quiero, por Dios, por favor, por Dios, no quiero, no podré soportarlo, por Dios…» El lenguaje se deshace en gimoteo. «Mirad en qué se ha convertido esta basura; en un cobarde. Quién te ha visto y quién te ve, Gutiérrez.» Aunque le hable a él, Michael Corleone, sin dejar de apuntarle, mira hacia sus propios hombres. «Tomad nota de lo que hacemos con los informantes y con los chivatos.» La cara de Gutiérrez se ha transformado en un nido de miedos, en una diana trémula: si el pistolero disparara, aunque el cañón esté a tan sólo medio centímetro del ojo derecho, es posible que la bala atravesara el tabique nasal, la ceja o el pómulo, tal es el grado de temblor de ese rostro desestructurado por el pavor.

«¿Qué ocurre? Llevas casi una hora tecleando sin parar.» «Estas páginas son chungas, en cuanto pones en los buscadores palabras clave como "mafia", "muerte", "crimen organizado", la cosa se complica, te va a costar cinco pavos más, pero te aseguro resultados.» Richie asiente: «¿Cuánto tiempo necesitas?». «Dame hasta mañana a primera hora.» «De acuerdo, pero ni se te ocurra jugármela.» «Descuida, me encanta saltarme la seguridad de la red y conseguir resultados; cuanto más difíciles, mejor.» «A primera hora.» «Sí, señor.»

«Se puede decir que durante todo el siglo xx el Gobierno controló la existencia de comunidades», afirma Lenny. «Hasta que llegó Internet», interviene Jessica. «Efectivamente.» Continúan en el sofá. La madrugada disuelve la oscuridad. Sobre la mesita de centro hay restos de pizza y de galletas, y varias tazas vacías. «Aunque ahora haya descubierto que todo era falso, que nunca conocí a Gaff, a Pris ni al resto, que sus imágenes y sus palabras llegaron a mis interferencias por sugestión, ¿entendéis?, por contagio, no me arrepiento de haber compartido con ellos todos estos años de…» «De terapia», completa Selena. «Sí», sonríe, «de terapia, de alivio, supongo que en el fondo pertenecer a una comunidad no es más que una forma de combatir la soledad.» «La soledad extrema», continúa Jessica, «que supone no tener vínculos sanguíneos, no compartir ADN, y sobre todo saber que la sangre y el ADN, teóricamente, se pueden compartir.»

Gutiérrez feels the soft texture of cement on his feet. He's standing, inside a one-cubic-meter container, with the barrel of a pistol on his right eye. 'You wouldn't die, but it would be very, very painful... There are people who remember how in the other life this type of death was called a Moe Green Special,' says the gunman. 'Michael, I don't understand why...' 'Mr Corleone! I've told you a thousand times that you have lost the right to call me by my first name, you fucking snitch.' Five suited men play the role of spectators or silent chorus around the two of them and the container full of cement. 'I don't want to go to the cemetery, for Chrissake, I don't want to join all the people I buried, I don't want to, please, I don't want to, I won't be able to bear it, for Chrissake...' His words crumble into a whimper. 'Just look what this piece of scum has turned into: a coward. Who'd have thought it, Gutiérrez.' Although he is still speaking to him, Michael Corleone, maintains his aim while he glances at his men. 'Remember what we do to pig informers and snitches.' Gutiérrez's face has become a pit of fear, a tremulous target: were the gunman to shoot, even if the barrel were half an inch away from his right eye, it's likely the bullet would go through his nose, eyebrow or cheekbone, such is the rate at which that face is shaking, collapsing from sheer terror.

'What's going on? You've been typing away for almost an hour.' 'It's tough with these pages, man. As soon as you search for words like "mafia", "death", "organised crime", it gets too hard. It's gonna cost you another five bucks, results guaranteed.' Richie nods. 'How long will it take?' 'Say, first thing tomorrow.' 'Ok, but no funny business.' 'Don't worry, I love hacking the web and getting results. The more difficult the search, the better.' 'First thing tomorrow.' 'Yes, sir.'

'You could say that the Government controlled the existence of communities throughout the twentieth century,' Lenny says. 'Until the internet came along,' Jessica chips in. 'That's right.' They are still on the couch. Morning dissolves darkness. Leftover pizza and cookies are on the coffee table as well as empty cups. 'Even though I discovered everything was fake, that I never really met Gaff, Pris or the others; even though their figures and their words entered my interferences through suggestion, you know? Through close contact, I still don't regret sharing all these years of...' 'Of therapy,' Selena finishes off. 'Yeah,' he smiles 'of therapy, relief... I guess that, ultimately, belonging to a community is simply a way of fighting loneliness.' 'Extreme loneliness,' Jessica adds, 'which implies not having any blood ties, not sharing DNA and, above all, knowing that blood and DNA, in theory, can be shared.'

Con el dedo índice, Nadia maximiza la ventana central de su pantalla. Es una cámara del puerto. Una grúa acaba de descargar un contenedor con número de localizador AE5089032. Lo teclea. Procede de los Emiratos Árabes. Cinco furgonetas grises metalizadas se alinean frente a la puerta del contenedor, que es abierta por un operario que no viste el uniforme reglamentario ni lleva casco. De cada vehículo descienden dos hombres fornidos, que empiezan a descargar cajas alargadas, de madera. Nadia manipula el zoom; el ordenador mide las cajas, las escanea, detecta en su interior la forma inconfundible de un misil tierra-aire. «Joder.» Toca dos veces la pantalla con el índice: aparece el mensaje «Enviar la información al centro superior de control»; toca dos veces más, «Muy urgente». La ventana se cierra.

La ventana se abre a renglón seguido en la pantalla central del Topo, que se está ajustando el nudo de la corbata en ese preciso instante. El Topo observa cómo las cajas son descargadas del contenedor y puestas, con cuidado, en la parte posterior de las furgonetas; cómo cierran las puertas de éstas; cómo sus ocupantes regresan a los asientos delanteros; cómo se ponen en marcha al tiempo que el contenedor vuelve a ser elevado por la grúa. Entonces dice por el micrófono: «Emergencia, emergencia, código 17: en el puerto de Nueva York, muelle 28, se está llevando a cabo una operación de descarga de armamento pesado; acudan inmediatamente todas las unidades disponibles». Su voz es recibida por una telefonista del Pentágono. Esta retransmite el mensaje a la comisaría del puerto. Cinco coches patrulla se ponen en marcha. Cuando llegan al muelle 28 es demasiado tarde: ya no hay nadie.

La puerta –parcial, móvil y doble como la de los salones de un western– se abre impulsada por el cuerpo de Richie Aprile. Observa panorámicamente el interior de los billares. Articulan el espacio dos filas, compuestas respectivamente por siete mesas de billar, cada una con una lámpara y varios tacos colgados de la pared. Al fondo hay una larga barra de bar, en cuyas cercanías algunos clientes apoyan sus traseros en taburetes con asiento de cuero negro. Sobre sus cabezas, cuatro televisores retransmiten espectáculos deportivos: béisbol, peleas de niños, competiciones de dardos, partidas de póquer. Richie Aprile atraviesa el pasillo central, mirando disimuladamente a las parejas y a los grupos de jugadores, que a su vez le observan, sin disimulo, con un punto de provocación. Se sienta en un extremo de la barra y pide una cerveza y unos nachos. Sus cinco últimos dólares. Ojea el periódico: «La Pandemia continúa siendo un misterio inexplicable. Hasta ahora ha afectado al 0,1 por ciento de la población mundial, según el comité especial de expertos». Al cabo de unos minutos le pregunta al barman: «¿Está por aquí Vito Spatafore?». «¿Quién pregunta?» «Alguien de la familia.» Entonces el barman, desde sus casi dos metros de altura, le hace un gesto a un jugador de billar de fisonomía asiática que, al acercarse, se convierte

Nadia uses her index finger to expand the central window on her screen. It's a camera in the port. A crane has just unloaded a container with the tracking number AE5089032. She types it in. It's from the Arab Emirates. Five metallic grey vans line up in front of the container door which a laborer opens who isn't wearing the regulation uniform or hard hat. Two brawny men jump out of each van and start unloading long wooden boxes. Nadia zooms in: the computer measures the boxes, scans them and detects the unmistakable shape of ground-to-air missiles. 'Fuck.' She touches the screen twice and the message 'Send information to Central Control' appears; she taps twice more, 'Urgent.' The window closes.

Immediately after the window opens on The Mole's central screen at the exact moment that he's adjusting the knot of his tie. The Mole watches as the boxes are unloaded from the container and placed carefully in the back of the vans; he watches as the doors are shut, as the men hop into the front seats; as the vans start up at the same time as the crane lifts the container back up. He speaks into the microphone: 'Emergency, emergency, Code 17: New York port, Pier 28: unloading of heavy weapons underway: all available units proceed to the scene immediately.' His message is received by the Pentagon switchboard and retransmitted to port security. Five patrol cars start up. When they get to Pier 28 it's too late: everyone's already gone.

Richie Aprile's body pushes open the double, swinging half-doors, like in a Wild West movie. His eyes pan across the inside of the pool hall. Two rows of seven pool tables fill the space, each with its own lamp and several cues hanging on the wall. There is a long bar at the back where several customers are resting their backsides on black-leather seated stools. Above their heads four televisions are broadcasting sport: baseball, kids boxing, darts competitions, poker games. Richie Aprile crosses the middle aisle, discreetly glancing at the couples and groups of pool players who look back at him not so discreetly, almost provocatively. He sits at one end of the bar and orders a beer and nachos. His last five dollars. He takes a look at the newspaper: The Pandemic remains an inexplicable mystery. According to the special committee of experts, 0.1 per cent of the world population has been affected so far. After a few minutes he asks the barman: 'Is Vito Spatafore around?' 'Who's asking?' 'I'm from the family.' From his height of almost six feet, the barman beckons to one of the pool players with Asian facial features. As the player approaches, it turns

en la única mujer del local. «Pregunta por ti, dice que es de la familia.» «Ah, ¿sí? Vaya, vaya... ¿Y qué familia es esa?», dice con una voz masculina que no desentona con su gestualidad ni con su cuerpo, equidistante entre los dos géneros. «La familia DiMeo.» Vito Spatafore abre exageradamente los ojos mientras dice: «Jack, déjanos el despacho». Desaparecen por una puerta que hay, disimulada, junto a los lavabos, en uno de los extremos de la barra.

Gutiérrez está inmerso en una mole sólida hasta los tobillos. Lo meten en una furgoneta. Lo llevan al puerto. Lo embarcan en un yate que pronto se interna en la bahía. Lo tiran por la borda. Cae, pesadamente. El agua difumina sus contornos. Cae, sigue cayendo. Hay peces. Se pierde la luz en la memoria del aire. Aterriza, con brusquedad líquida, en pie, sobre la arena del fondo. Se levanta una nube de polvo acuático que tarda algunos segundos en disgregarse. Tiene los ojos abiertos, respira, de vez en cuando alguna burbuja escapa de sus labios. Puede mover los brazos, el torso, la cadera: pero los pies están atrapados por el bloque de cemento. Se da cuenta de que no está solo. A su lado hay un hombre de unos sesenta años, el cuerpo arrugadísimo, los ojos muy abiertos, la mirada asustada. Como un pez cuya cola hubiera sido adherida al fondo de la pecera. Y otro. Y una mujer. Y otra. Diez, veinte, cincuenta. Un centenar de cadáveres en vida rodean a Gutiérrez en su nueva prisión: su mundo nuevo. Un centenar de ojos de pez se giran para mirarle, desorbitados por un pánico constante.

«También nuestra comunidad ha crecido exponencialmente», dice Nadia por el micrófono, «hasta el punto de que ahora el Gobierno no puede contratar a todos los que están convencidos de haber trabajado para nosotros en el más allá, por eso han proliferado las redes alternativas y las asociaciones ilícitas... Esto se acaba, amigo mío, esto se acaba... Si no lo hace la epidemia, lo haremos nosotros mismos.» La voz de Frank suena irónica en los altavoces: «Cariño, si esto es el puto apocalipsis, me pido pasarlo contigo en un jacuzzi, con velas y champán». «Ay, Frank, eres incorregible.» «Hablando en serio, Nadia.» Ella se concentra en la ventana de su pantalla donde se ve la furgoneta negra. «Creo que pronto voy a necesitar tu ayuda, esta nueva cámara va a dar resultados muy, pero que muy pronto.»

«Jack, avisa a los chicos», dice Vito Spatafore sacando apenas la cabeza por la ranura de la puerta. El barman avisa a los tres hombres que estaban jugando a billar con ella. En cuanto entran en el despacho (una gran mesa llena de papelotes, un pequeño escritorio con un ordenador, siete sillas, una máquina expendedora de tabaco, una diana con tres dardos, tres pósteres pornográficos), Vito les dice: «Os presento a alguien de la familia. Todavía no sabe cómo se llama, pero he hablado mucho con él, y no hay duda de

out to be the only woman in the hall. 'He's asking for you, says he's from the family.' 'Oh yeah? Which family might that be?' she asks with a masculine voice that is in sync with her gestures and her body, mid-way between the two genders. 'The Di Meo family.' Vito Spatafore widens her eyes exaggeratedly as she says, 'Jack, let us use the office.' They disappear through a concealed door next to the restrooms at the far end of the bar.

Gutiérrez is up to his ankles in a concrete block up. They put him in a van. They take him to the harbor. They put him on a yacht that soon goes deeper into the bay. They throw him overboard. He sinks heavily. The water blurs the outline of his body. He goes down and down. There are fish. The light fades into the air's memory. He lands on his feet on the sandy bottom with a liquid thud. A cloud of watery particles rises up that takes a few seconds to disperse. His eyes are open, he breathes, and from time to time a bubble escapes from his lips. He can move his arms, torso and hips, but his feet are trapped in the concrete block. He realizes he's not alone. Next to him is a man around sixty with a very wrinkled body, eyes wide open in terror. Like a fish stuck by the tail to the bottom of a fish tank. And another. And a woman. And another woman. Ten, twenty, fifty. A hundred living corpses surround Gutierrez in his new prison, his new world. A hundred fish eyes turn to watch him, their eyes popping out in permanent panic.

'Our community has increased exponentially,' says Nadia over the microphone, 'to the point where now the Government cannot hire all of those who are convinced they worked for us in the other life. For that reason, alternative networks and illegal groups have proliferated. It's nearly over, my friend. It's nearly over. If the epidemic doesn't do it, we'll do it ourselves.' Frank's voice sounds ironic over the loudspeakers. 'If this is the mother-fuckin' apocalypse, honey, I want to spend it with you in a Jacuzzi with candles and champagne.' 'Oh, Frank, you're incorrigible.' 'But seriously, Nadia.' She focuses on the black van just appearing on her screen. 'I believe I'm soon going to need your help. This new camera is going to get results, and really soon.'

'Jack! Call the boys,' says Vito Spatafore, hardly sticking his head out of the half open door. The barman calls the three men who were playing pool with her. As soon as they get to the office (a big table littered with papers, a small computer desk, seven chairs, a cigarette vending machine, a dartboard with three darts stuck on it, three porno posters), Vito says, 'I want to introduce you to a member of our family. He still doesn't know his name, but I have talked to him a lot and there is no doubt

que es uno de los nuestros». Sandro, Carlo y Christopher le dan la mano. Este último, rubio y de ojos azules, le dice mientras se estrechan las manos: «Ya te habrá dicho Vito que estamos en un momento complicado. Cuantos más seamos, mejor». «Todavía no le he hablado del tema Corleone, habrá tiempo, Chris, habrá tiempo.» Vito se da la vuelta y los tres hombres admiran sus nalgas, la única parte de su cuerpo que, al moverse, se revela absolutamente femenina. De la caja fuerte que hay en la pared, junto a un cuadro que representa figuras borrosas y cenicientas, extrae una botella de licor y cinco vasos. Sirve. Brindan. Exclaman: «Salute!». (105–110)

that he is one of us.' Sandro, Carlo and Christopher shake his hand. The latter, blond and blue-eyed, shakes his hand and says: 'Vito must have already told you that we are in a difficult situation. The more we are, the better. I still haven't talked to him about the Corleone business, we have time, Chris, we have time.' Vito turns around and the three men look admiringly at his buttocks, the only part of his body that, as it moves, reveals itself to be completely feminine. She grabs a liquor bottle and five glasses from a safe in the wall, by a painting of some blurry, ash-grey figures. He serves, they toast and exclaim: '*Salute.*'

Chapter 10

The missing king

Written by Moetai Brotherson

Translated by Laura Ruch, Patricia Worth, Sally Carlton, Genevieve Fahey,
Anne-Marie Garrioch, Nicole McLean, Melissa McMahon, Brigitte Miles,
Nadia Niaz and Heather Pye

Led by Jean Anderson

Published in 2007 (Pape'ete: Au Vent des îles), Moetai Brotherson's *Le Roi absent* is the story of a gifted mute, Vaki (also known as Heremanu and Moanam), from the Marquesas. It begins as a typical postcolonial success story – Vaki travels to France, enjoys success there, and returns to Tahiti an aeronautical engineer – until disaster strikes and Vaki must serve prison time for a crime he did not commit. After his death, Vaki's psychologist takes up the search for the unexplained origins of Vaki's non-Tahitian name, Moanam. The novel is part thriller, part quixotic search and part flight of imagination. Brotherson plays with the conventional (colonial) Bildungsroman structure and his style borrows from multiple narrative traditions, while Vaki's muteness can be seen as emblematic of the Mā'ohi people. Jean Anderson's translation of *Le Roi absent* is to be published in 2012 by Little Island Press (Auckland).

Le Roi absent

Le fils Weiller et une certaine Maggy font figure d'épouvantails. Ils sont très différents cependant. L'un est roux, très blanc et semble avoir été élevé en laboratoire. L'autre est très brune, d'allure sportive, avec un accent métropolitain qui tranche avec son physique bien de chez nous. Les regards que nous échangeons me rappellent les westerns du dimanche après-midi. Flanqués de nos bottes à éperons, la main en alerte maximale, le pas arqué soulevant la poussière rouge, nous avançons. Vetea et moi d'un côté de la rue, Weiller et Maggy à l'opposé. À l'ombre de nos larges chapeaux les regards ne doivent révéler aucune émotion, aucun énervement : le duel est psychologique avant tout. Les portes et les volets se ferment à notre passage. Les petits enfants dans la rue sont happés par des mains secourables qui les mettent à l'abri. Le piano du saloon s'est tu : la boucherie va commencer...

Les parties se succèdent et se ressemblent pour nous quatre. Nos adversaires ne font pas le poids. À midi, lorsque la première partie du tournoi s'achève, nous sommes tous les quatre en quarts de finale. Pause déjeuner. Je ne quitte pas Vetea d'une semelle comme me l'a conseillé mon oncle. La Maggy a bien essayé de venir s'asseoir à notre table mais nous l'avons chassée du regard. Avant la reprise du tournoi, nous allons nous promener du côté de la marina. Assis près de l'eau nous observons un groupe d'adolescents assis en cercle fumant un joint.

– Tu vois ça Vaki, c'est de la drogue, c'est pas bien, c'est la Bible qui le dit.

Il a un côté prédicateur un peu énervant quand il s'y met Vetea. Pour lui faire plaisir je hoche la tête. Il faudra que je lise la Bible un jour pour vérifier ce qu'il me raconte. Je repense à grand-mère Nuku. On m'a dit qu'elle était morte le lendemain du mariage de la cousine Hélène. Ça m'a fait tout drôle. Je m'en suis voulu car j'ai pensé qu'elle s'était épuisée à venir me parler dans la porcherie.

Quatorze heures trente, nous reprenons le chemin du lycée en passant par le stade de football. Devant nous, à une centaine de mètres, une fille va également en direction du lycée. C'est la première fois que mon regard s'attarde sur un corps de fille. C'est joli finalement quand ça grandit un peu, presque élégant ; sauf qu'elle fait des tout petits pas : totalement stupide. La preuve, à l'arrivée, elle a fait un total de huit cent soixante-dix-huit pas, alors que moi, en augmentant sensiblement ma foulée, j'ai réduit ce nombre à six cent treize. Et là, je ne compte même pas la portion de chemin avant le stade de foot...

The missing king

The young Weiller and a certain Maggy are the ones to worry about. They are, however, very different. He's a redhead, very pale, and looks as if he's been raised in a laboratory. She's a brunette, sporty-looking with a European accent that doesn't go with her 'Islander' looks. We exchange stares that remind me of Sunday afternoon westerns. Vetea and I advance from one end of the street, Weiller and Maggy from the other – our spurred boots stir up the red dust, trigger fingers are twitching, as we go. From the shadow of our cowboy hats, our eyes must not reveal any emotion, any sign of nerves: above all else, the duel is psychological. Doors and shutters close as we go by. Little children in the street are snatched up by rescuing hands, bundled off to safety. The piano in the saloon stops playing. The slaughter is about to begin.

Game after game brings the same result for the four of us. Our opponents aren't up to scratch. At midday as the first part of the tournament comes to an end, the four of us have made it through to the quarter finals. Lunch break. I stick close to Vetea the way my uncle told me to. The girl Maggy did try to sit at our table but we glared her away. Before the tournament starts again we go for a walk near the marina. Sitting beside the water, we watch a group of teenagers sitting in a circle and smoking a joint.

'See that Vaki, they're doing drugs, that's not good, that's what the Bible says.'

There's a preachy side to him that's a bit annoying once he gets going, Vetea. I nod to make him feel good. I'm going to have to read the Bible again one day to check up on what he's telling me. I think about Grandmother Nuku again. They told me she died the day after my cousin Hélène's wedding. It made me feel really weird. I was mad at myself, thinking that she must have worn herself out coming to speak to me in the pigpen.

Two-thirty, we head back to the school, walking past the football stadium. About a hundred metres in front of us there's a girl who is also going towards the school. It's the first time I have really looked at a girl's body. They're kind of pretty when they grow up a bit, almost elegant; except she's taking very tiny steps, how completely stupid. Obviously, because by the time she gets there she has taken eight hundred and seventy-eight steps, whereas I have cut that down to six hundred and thirteen by lengthening my stride a bit. And that's not even counting the part before the football stadium...

Nous voici au stade des demi-finales. Vetea affronte Weiller et moi je joue contre une fille. Une fille ! C'est la première fois que je joue contre une fille. Vetea s'est bien battu, mais la souris de laboratoire l'a mis mat au vingt-septième coup. Voilà ce que c'est de faire de la programmation au lieu de s'entraîner. Maggy joue comme le niveau huit de Chessmaster, avec des ouvertures grosses comme ça mais une défense solide basée sur la combinaison tour-cavalier. Je l'observe, elle est bourrée de tics. Elle se mordille la lèvre inférieure, elle se triture le lobe de l'oreille, elle tire sur son nez comme si elle voulait l'allonger. Je viens de prendre sa tour, elle a l'air très contrariée, je sens qu'elle a les larmes au bord des yeux. Elle prend son temps et moi, je compte ses cils. Quarante-trois sur la paupière droite, quarante et un sur la gauche. Je n'ai jamais trouvé quelqu'un qui ait le même nombre de cils sur les deux. Tout à coup je sens son regard intrigué sur moi. Elle pense que je la regarde ! Idiote, je compte tes cils, ai-je envie de lui dire.

Non mais, pour qui se prend-elle ? Elle se met à me faire des petits battements des yeux tout en souriant. Ah, elle veut jouer ? Elle me croit stupide ? Dans les six coups qui ont suivi, j'ai perdu mes deux tours, un fou et un cavalier. Elle est ravie. Elle ne sait pas que je peux la battre avec mes pions. Quarante-huitième coup, elle est mat et ne comprend pas pourquoi ! Ça devrait être interdit d'échecs les filles...

C'est la pause. Avec mes grimaces et ma gestuelle codifiée je passe un savon à Vetea qui s'excuse. Pas d'excuses ! Vetea s'en va, contrarié. Cinq minutes plus tard, je retrouve mon ami, mon seul ami. Pardon l'ami. Ce n'est qu'un jeu après tout. Mais quand même... Weiller est encore plongé dans son gros bouquin noir quand on nous rappelle pour la finale. Je jette un coup d'œil à l'ouvrage : *Échecs, les 500 meilleures ouvertures*. Retour dans la rue de terre rouge. L'ambiance est électrique. Frappé en plein cœur, Vetea gît face contre terre près de l'entrée du coiffeur. Maggy est assise, une balle entre les deux yeux qui continuent de cligner dans les derniers sursauts.

Weiller fait le premier pas. Pion blanc en e4. Pion noir juste en face. Cavalier blanc en f3. Cavalier noir juste en face. Je sens que ça l'énerve. Il se demande si je réfléchis ou si je me contente de copier ses coups. Il prend mon pion en e5 avec son cavalier. Là je rigole : pion noir en d6. Son cavalier bat en retraite, le mien venge mon pion en prenant e4. Je sens qu'il hésite, il est sur la défensive, il protège son roi et moi je lui mets la pression au centre. Neuvième coup, cavalier noir en b4, échec à la reine. Il se replie en e2. Dix-huitième coup, il me croit faible et pour l'en convaincre je sors ma reine en d7. Il s'engouffre et fait pression. Il cherche à isoler mon roi. Il y perd son cavalier en d6 au

Now, we've reached the semi-finals. Vetea is up against Weiller. I'm playing against a girl. A girl! It's the first time I've ever played against a girl. Vetea fought hard, but the lab rat checkmated him on the twenty-seventh move. That's what you get for doing programming when you ought to be training. Maggy plays like Chessmaster level eight, with huge opening moves but a solid defence based on the rook-knight combination. I watch her, she's ticcing all over the place. She chews on her bottom lip, fiddles with her ear lobe, pulls at her nose as if she's trying to make it longer. I've just taken her rook, she looks pretty cross, I can tell she's close to tears. She takes her time while I count her eyelashes. Forty-three on her right eyelid, forty one on the left. I've never seen anyone with the same number on both. Suddenly I can feel her looking at me, intrigued. She thinks I'm staring at her! Idiot, I nearly say, I'm counting your eyelashes.

No really, who does she think she is? She starts to smile and bat her eyelashes at me. Right, so she wants to play, does she? Does she think I'm stupid? Six more moves and I've lost both my rooks, a bishop and a knight. She's really pleased. She doesn't know I can beat her with my pawns. Maggy is checkmated on the forty-eighth move and can't understand why! Girls just shouldn't be allowed to play chess...

It's the break. I pull faces and use coded gestures to give Vetea a good telling-off. He makes excuses. No excuses! Vetea goes off, peeved. Five minutes later I go looking for my friend, my only friend. Sorry, friend. It's only a game, after all. But, even so... Weiller still has his nose buried in his big black book when they call us in for the final. I take a quick look at the book: *Chess, the Best 500 Openings*. Back to the red dirt of the street. The atmosphere is electric. Shot through the heart, Vetea is lying face down on the ground near the barber's door. Maggy is sitting there, a bullet between the eyes, still fluttering in their death throes.

Weiller makes the first move. White pawn to e4. Black pawn opposite. White knight to f3. Black knight opposite. I can tell he's getting annoyed. He's not sure whether I'm thinking or if I'm just copying his moves. He takes my pawn at e5 with his knight. Now I'm laughing; black pawn to d6. His knight beats a retreat, mine avenges my pawn by taking e4. I can tell he's hesitant, he's on the defensive, protecting his king, and at the centre I put pressure on him. Ninth move, black knight to b4, check to the queen. He skulks back to e2. Eighteenth move, he thinks I'm weak and to convince him I send my queen out to d7. He charges in and turns the pressure up. He tries to isolate my king but ends up losing his knight at d6 on the

vingt et unième coup. Trente-troisième coup. Nouvelle ruée blanche. Il n'obtient que mon pion. Quand je décide d'échanger nos dames, au quarantième coup il se rend compte que j'ai l'avantage. Mais il a de la ressource. Quarante-troisième coup, son cavalier vient défier mon roi en f7. Il poursuit sa chasse mais finit par se lasser. Cinquante-quatrième coup, la fin est proche, je décide de l'accélérer en procédant à l'échange des tours. Mon cavalier prend son roi en chasse. Il se déplace, puis cherche à me bloquer. Il en oublie mes pions qui continuent d'avancer et ma tour placée en embuscade. Soixantième coup, son fou a rattrapé mon cavalier en b1. Il sourit. Bel optimisme, de courte durée. Je viens d'amener ma tour en c3. Il réalise qu'il ne pourra pas empêcher mes deux pions en a5 et b4 d'être reines. Ma tour va faire un carnage dans ses troupes. Il pose ses mains de part et d'autre de l'échiquier. Il couche son roi. Il aura tenu soixante et un coups. Je ne suis pas fier de moi. Dans notre camp c'est l'explosion, et la consternation chez nos adversaires. Je rajuste mon chapeau, souffle dans le canon de mon six-coups. Weiller, debout, regarde incrédule le trou dans sa poitrine. Il est tombé, le tueur de légende. (48–52)

twenty-first move. Thirty-third move. Renewed white onslaught. He only gets my pawn. When I decide to exchange our queens, he realises on the fortieth move that I have the upper hand. But he still has some moves up his sleeve. Forty-third move, his knight threatens my king at f7.

He keeps after me but runs out of steam. Fifty-fourth move, the end is near. I decide to speed things up by exchanging rooks. My knight goes after his king. He moves away, then tries to block me. He has forgotten about my pawns that continue to advance. He has forgotten my rook that is set up in ambush. Sixtieth move, his bishop catches up with my knight at b1. He smiles. Such optimism, for such a short time. I've just moved my rook to c3. He realizes that he cannot stop my two pawns at a5 and b4 from becoming queens. My rook is going to wreak havoc amongst his troops! He places one hand on each side of the chessboard. He lays down his king. He lasted sixty-one moves. I am not proud of myself. In our camp, there is an explosion of joy. Our opponents are distraught. I settle my hat, blow into the barrel of my six-shooter. Weiller, standing, stares incredulously at the hole in his chest. It's curtains for the legendary killer.

Chapter 11

Like a bird in a cage

Written by Heike Brandt

Translated by Meaghan Bruce, Tomas Drevikovsky, Peggy Ludt-Nash, Joachim Redner, Juliane Roemhild and Pauline Rogan

Led by Heike Brandt and Elizabeth Honey

Edited by Rosalind Price

First published in 1992, only a few years after the fall of the Berlin Wall, Heike Brandt's *Wie ein Vogel im Käfig* (Beltz & Gelberg) tells the story of 16-year-old Petra, a high-school student living in the Berlin suburb of Kreuzberg. Petra has endured years of sexual abuse committed by her father, but she becomes tangled in a web of lies, instead accusing her school friend Halef of the atrocious deed. Petra's friend Rebecca narrates this moving story, which explores the themes of friendship, sexuality, ethnicity and family. Brandt's use of language, including German 'youth speak', Turkish, Turkish German and the Berlin dialect, make this text particularly challenging for translators.

Wie ein Vogel im Käfig

Zwischen Fabian und mir herrscht Grabesstille. Ich habe ihm erzählt, was ich von Petra weiß. Für mich gibt es nun nicht den Hauch eines Zweifels mehr. Ich habe ihm natürlich nicht alles im Detail gesagt - das hätte ich gar nicht fertig gebracht -, aber er hat's auch so begriffen. Hat mich mit grollen Augen angeguckt, richtig bestürzt. Und dann hat er leise gesagt: „Trotzdem - solange Halef es nicht zugibt, glaube ich ihm. Ich kann mir das einfach nicht vorstellen, dass er so gemein sein kann. Ich kenne ihn schon so lange. Und im Grunde hasst er seinen Vater, weil der so brutal zu seiner Mutter ist. So einer kann doch dann nicht selber ein Monster werden. Das geht mir einfach nicht in den Kopf."

Irgendwo muss es Grenzen geben, auch bei der besten Freundschaft. Ich kann nicht begreifen, dass Fabian nicht wenigstens versucht, mehr aus Halef rauszukriegen. Als ob er die Augen zumacht, sich die Ohren verstopft, weil einfach nicht sein kann, was nicht sein darf. So eine Haltung lehne ich ab. Ich rede nicht mehr mit ihm. Und Halefs Familie gehe ich auf keinen Fall mehr besuchen. Es stimmt nicht, was Ruth gesagt hat. Die Mütter erziehen schließlich ihre Söhne, ein bisschen Verantwortung haben die auch. An Kuckuckseier glaube ich nicht. Eine Sache will mir nicht aus dem Kopf. Was ist, wenn Petra schwanger ist von Halef? Das kann doch sein, oder? Kinder können auch ohne Liebe gezeugt werden, da bin ich mir verdammt sicher. (143–144)

„Komm doch mit, Tee trinken", schlägt Gülay vor. „Du warst so lange nicht mehr bei mir. Bitte!"

Natürlich reden wir über Halef und Petra. Gülay hat zwar davon gehört, weiß aber nichts Genaues.

„Eh, das kann doch nicht sein!", sagt sie schließlich. „Das kann überhaupt nicht wahr sein!"

„Was?", frage ich verunsichert. Zweifelt sie an Petras Aussage? Hält sie zu Halef?

„Das Ganze! Das ist doch verrückt. Da stimmt was nicht!"

„Ach, Gülay. Schön wär's ja. Aber es ist nun mal passiert, so und nicht anders. Ich kapier's ja auch nicht."

Hüseyin kommt nach Hause. Der Blaumann steht ihm wirklich gut, er sieht aus wie ein Profi. Er verschwindet gleich im Bad, um sich zu waschen und frische Sachen anzuziehen. „Gülay, wo ist meine Hose?", ruft er. „Ein Hemd brauche ich auch!"

Gülay steht auf und holt ihm das Zeug.

„He, spinnst du?", sage ich. „Du bist doch nicht sein Dienstmädchen!"

Like a bird in a cage

A deathly silence hangs over Fabian and me. I've told him what Petra said. There's not a shadow of doubt left, as far as I'm concerned. Naturally I didn't tell him every detail – I don't think I could have – but he still got it. He stared at me, eyes wide, truly horrified. And then he said softly, "Still – as long as Halef doesn't admit to it, I'll believe him. I just can't imagine he could be so mean. I've known him for ages. Basically he hates his father for being violent to his mother. Someone like that doesn't just turn into a monster himself. I can't get my head around it."

There's got to be a limit somewhere, even in the best of friendships. It beats me that Fabian doesn't even try to get more out of Halef. Like he's shutting his eyes and blocking his ears, as if that which must not, can not be. I simply can't accept an attitude like that. I'm not talking to him anymore. And no way am I going to visit Halef's family again. What Ruth said isn't true. After all, mothers bring up their sons; they have to take some responsibility. Halef is no cuckoo in the nest. There's one thing I can't get out of my head, though. What if he's got Petra pregnant? It's possible, isn't it? You can conceive children without love, I'm damn sure about that…

"Come home with me and have some tea," Gülay suggests. "It's ages since you've been to my place. Come on!"

We talk about Halef and Petra, of course. Gülay has heard about it, but she doesn't know any details.

"That can't be right!" she says finally. "That can't possibly be true!"

"What?" Now I'm confused. Does she doubt Petra's statement? Is she on Halef's side?

"The whole thing! It's just crazy. Something's not right!"

"Ah, Gülay. If only. That's the way it happened, though; I don't get it either."

Hüseyin comes home. The blue overalls really suit him; he looks professional. He ducks straight into the bathroom to wash and change into clean clothes.

"Gülay, where are my pants?" he yells. "I need a shirt too."

Gülay stands up and gets him his things.

"Hey, are you crazy?" I say. "You're not his maid, are you?"

„Wenn der an den Schrank rangeht, dann schmeißt er bloß alles durcheinander", lacht sie.

Schließlich kommen auch die Eltern. Sie arbeiten beide in einer Metallfabrik. Die Mutter verschwindet gleich in der Küche, das Abendessen vorbereiten.

„Na, meine Tochter", begrüßt mich Gülays Vater Ali. „Endlich mal wieder hier? Wie geht's dir? Was macht deine Mutter?" Seiner Tochter gibt er einen Kuss, dann klopft er an die Badezimmertür. „Mach schon, ich will mich waschen."

„Du bleibst doch zum Essen?", fragt Gülay. Warum nicht. Zu Hause ist sowieso nichts los. „Dann komm mit in die Küche."

Gülays Mutter Gönül küsst mich auf beide Wangen. „Na, wie geht's dir? Alles klar?"

„Alles klar. Und dir?"

„Ach, danke. Scheißfabrikarbeit. Immer Kopfschmerzen. *Erol nerede, Gülay?*"

„Auf dem Hof."

„*Onu çağir Yirkansın.*"

Gülay ruft in den Hof hinunter und ihr kleiner Bruder Erol kommt auch sofort hoch. Er sieht aus wie ein Bauarbeiter, verdreckt von oben bis unten.

Die Mutter erwischt ihn gleich an der Tür und schimpft sofort los: „Wie siehst du aus? Scheißedreck! Was hast du gemacht, he?"

„Ich hab gespielt, *anne*, da war ..."

Sie lässt ihn gar nicht ausreden, sondern zerrt ihm grob die Sachen vom Leib. „Was sollen die Leute denken, du? Scheißetürken, immer dreckig, oder wie? Mein Sohn Schwein, oder wie? Alle Deutschen denken, Türken Schweine. Und Sachen gehen kaputt, Mama neue kaufen, was?" Und dann kippt sie noch einen Schwall auf Türkisch hinterher. Sie ist völlig außer sich, der Junge weiß gar nicht, wie ihm geschieht.

„*Anne*, jetzt hör doch auf!", sagt Gülay. „Das geht doch in der Wäsche wieder raus."

Endlich hat sich Erol aus dem Griff seiner Mutter gewunden und verschwindet im Kinderzimmer. Er heult wütend.

Als das Essen auf dem Wohnzimmertisch steht, hat sich die Stimmung wieder beruhigt. Erol, dem Jüngsten, kann sowieso keiner lange böse sein.

Es gibt Linsensuppe - rote, passierte Linsen, mit Zitrone abgeschmeckt -, Lammfleisch mit Kartoffeln in einer dünnen Soße, gemischten Salat mit viel Petersilie und dazu jede Menge Brot. Den Salat essen wir gemeinsam von der flachen Schale, das andere Essen bekommt jeder einzeln auf einem Teller serviert. Dazu läuft der Fernseher, türkisches Programm.

Vorhin hab ich mit Gülay darüber gesprochen, ob sie nicht Lust hat, mit nach Italien zu kommen. Jetzt ist ein günstiger Moment zu fragen.

"If he goes to the cupboard he'll only mess everything up," she says with a laugh. Her parents, who work in a sheet-metal factory, come home. Her mother disappears into the kitchen to cook dinner.

Gülay's father Ali welcomes me. "Hello, my daughter. Good to see you again – it's been a while. How are you? How's your mother getting on?" He kisses Gülay, then knocks on the bathroom door. "Hurry up, I want to have a wash."

"You are staying for dinner, aren't you?" Gülay asks.

Why not. There's nothing going on at home, anyway.

"Come on into the kitchen."

Gülay's mother kisses me on both cheeks. "So, how are you? All good?"

"All good. How about you?"

She sighs. "Thanks. Bloody factory job. Always headache. *Erol, nerede, Gülay?*"

"In the yard."

"*Onu çaðýr. Yirkansýn.*"

Gülay calls down, and her little brother Erol comes up right away. He looks like a builder's labourer, covered in dirt from head to toe.

His mother catches him at the door and lets him have it. "Look at you! Bloody crap dirt! What you been up to, eh?"

"I was playing, *anne*, there was ..."

She tears off his clothes without even letting him finish. "What will people think, eh? Dirty Turks, always dirty, huh? My son pig, huh? All Germans think Turks pigs. And clothes get kaput, Mama buy new or what?" She tops it off with a torrent of Turkish. She is completely beside herself – the boy doesn't know what's hit him.

"*Anne*, please, give it a rest," Gülay says. "The dirt'll wash out."

Erol finally wriggles free from his mother's grip and disappears into the kids' room, so angry he starts crying.

By the time dinner is on the coffee table, things have calmed down. Erol's the youngest; nobody can stay angry with him for long.

There's lentil soup – pureed red lentils, with lemon – lamb with potatoes in a light sauce, mixed salad with lots of parsley, and plenty of bread to go with it. We all share the salad from a platter, and get the other food served on our own plates. In the background the TV is on – a Turkish channel.

Earlier, I had asked Gülay whether she wanted to come to Italy too. Now is a good time to bring it up.

„Ali *amca*", sage ich, das heißt Onkel Ali. Ich weiß, dass er sich über diese Anrede freut. „Wir wollen im Sommer mit den Falken nach Italien fahren. Darf Gülay mit?"

„Ich will auch mit!", kräht Erol.

„Halt die Klappe!" Gülay stößt ihn in die Seite.

„Falken? Was ist das?", fragt Gülays Mutter.

„Eine Jugendorganisation."

„Jungenorganisation? Kommt gar nicht in die Tüte!",

sagt Ali *amca* und grinst dabei.

„Papa, du bist doof. Hör doch mal richtig hin! Jugend! Da fahren lauter Jugendliche mit. Aber mit Betreuern."

„Und auch Jungen, was?"

„Aber auch viele Mädchen", sage ich.

„Nee, nee, das ist zu gefährlich!"

„Mensch, Papa! Die Reise ist ganz billig! Und drei Wochen lang Italien. Ich wollte schon immer mal nach Italien. *Anne*, sag du doch mal was!"

„Ich weiß nicht. Wir wollen doch in die Türkei."

„Ach, immer in die Türkei. Und aufs Dorf. Ist doch langweilig. Bitte, Papa!"

„Aber was ist mit den Jungen?"

„Ach, Ali *amca*, die machen doch nichts. Ich darf doch auch mit."

„Dann soll Hüseyin mitfahren und aufpassen."

„Ich bin doch nicht blöd!", braust Hüseyin auf. „Die kann auf sich alleine aufpassen. Außerdem habe ich in der Zeit gar keinen Urlaub."

Ali schüttelt den Kopf. „Also, ich weiß ja nicht ..."

„Also ja!", jubelt Gülay. „Ja, *anne*?"

„Mal abwarten." (147–151)

"Ali *amca*," I say, which means uncle Ali. I know he loves being called that. "We are planning to go to Italy with the *Falken* this summer. Can Gülay come?"

"I wanna come too!," squawks Erol.

"Shut up!" Gülay elbows him in the ribs.

"*Falken*? What's that?" Gülay's mother asks.

"A youth organisation."

"Youths? You mean boys? No way!" Ali amca says with a grin.

"Papa, don't be silly. Listen carefully! Youth! It's all kids. But supervised."

"Boys, too, eh?"

"And lots of girls," I say.

"No, no, that's too risky."

"Come on, Papa! The trip is really cheap. Three weeks in Italy. I've always wanted to go to Italy. *Anne* – why don't you say something!"

"Well, I don't know. We all wanted to go to Turkey."

"Ugh, Turkey again! Back to the village. So boring. Papa, please!"

"And what about those boys?"

"Huh, Ali *amca*, they won't do anything. After all, *I'm* allowed to go."

"Then Hüseyin will go along to keep an eye on you."

"You think I'm stupid?" Hüseyin bursts out. "She can look after herself. And anyway, I don't get holidays at that time."

Ali shakes his head. "Well, I still don't know …"

"So it's yes, then!" Gülay cheers. "Yes, *Anne*?"

"We'll see."

Contributors' biographies

Jean Anderson is Associate Professor of French at Victoria University of Wellington, New Zealand, where she founded the New Zealand Centre for Literary Translation/Te Tumu Whakawhiti Tuhinga o Aotearoa in 2007. She has been a literary translator since 2004 (French–English; co-translations English–French), and has since published 11 books and over 100 short pieces of prose and poetry, in New Zealand, France, French Polynesia, the US and the UK. Her most recent books are Ananda Devi's *Indian Tango* (Host, 2011) and substantial contributions to a collection of short stories featuring food, *French Feast* (Whereabouts Press, 2011).

Heike Brandt (64) lives in Berlin as an author, translator and reviewer of literature for young people. She has studied pedagogy and has worked for 10 years in a collectively owned and run bookstore for children's literature. She is engaged in Redistribute! Foundation for one world in solidarity, which promotes intercultural learning for young people with or without migration backgrounds by travelling together, especially to Turkey.

Moetai Brotherson was born in Papeete, Tahiti, French Polynesia and started writing at the age of 14. He has written eight novels, three books of poetry and two children's books. He published *Le Roi absent* with Au vent des îles, Papeete, in June 2007: it took the Tahitian literary world by storm, and remains a bestseller in French Polynesia. He has also published articles in the literary magazine *Literamâ'ohi*, with excerpts from *Le Roi absent* appearing in the English postcolonial literary magazine *Wasafiri* in 2010. In 2009, *Le Roi absent* was awarded the highly coveted University of French Polynesia prize. The translation, 'The Missing King', will be published by Little Island Books (Auckland) in 2012.

Peter Bush is an award-winning literary translator who now lives in Barcelona. He was previously Professor of Literary Translation at the University of East Anglia and Director of the British Centre for Literary Translation. Recent translations from Spanish include *Níjar Country* and *Exiled from Almost Everywhere* by Juan Goytisolo, and *Desolation Island* by Adolfo García Ortega. Translations from Catalan include *A Shortcut to*

Paradise by Teresa Solana and *Guadalajara* by Quim Monzó. Peter is now finishing *Tyrant Banderas* by Ramón del Valle-Inclán, the classic novel on the theme of Hispanic dictatorships, and *The Gray Notebook* by Josep Pla, the first translation of this Catalan masterpiece of autobiographical writing.

Jorge Carrión holds a Ph.D. in comparative literature from Universidad Pompeu Fabra, where he teaches creative writing and contemporary literature at undergraduate and graduate levels. A writer and literary critic, he has published several travel books, a novel, *Los Muertos* (Mondadori, 2011), and two essays: *Viaje contra espacio* (Iberoamericana, 2008) and *Teleshakespeare* (Errate Naturae, 2011).

Adele D'Arcangelo is a tenured lecturer-researcher at the SSLiMIT-University of Bologna (Faculty for Interpreters and Translators based in Forlì), where she teaches English–Italian translation. Her research interests include literary and multimedia translation and translation teaching. She has published articles on intercultural communication, literary translation, and translation and the media (especially theatre translation and translation of comics). She has translated works by Samuel Beckett, Alan Bennett and Steven Berkoff, among others.

Dr Leah Gerber completed her Ph.D. in German Studies at Monash University in 2008. Her doctoral thesis 'Tracing a Tradition: German Translations of Australian Children's Fiction 1945 to the Present' explored the strategies adopted by translators of children's literature, as distinct from adult literature, as well as the translation of 'Australianness'. She has published widely in the area of children's literary translation and has co-authored a number of research projects in the area of translation and interpreting service provision in Victoria. She has worked as a lecturer in translation and interpreting studies at Monash University since 2009 and is director of the Literary Translation Winter School and Festival.

Dr Valerie Henitiuk is Senior Lecturer in Literature and Translation and Director of the British Centre for Literary Translation at the University of East Anglia (UK). *Embodied Boundaries*, on liminal metaphor in English, French and Japanese appeared in 2007, and *Worlding Sei Shônagon: The Pillow Book in Translation* has just been published by University of Ottawa Press. A co-edited collection of short stories by women from India's Orissa province appeared in 2010; another co-edited volume on the work of

W. G. Sebald is forthcoming from Manchester University Press. Her work has also been published in the *Canadian Review of Comparative Literature*, *Comparative Literature Studies*, *META*, *Translation Studies* and *TTR*, and in collected volumes such as *Teaching World Literature* (MLA 2009), *Thinking through Translation with Metaphors* (St Jerome 2010) and *Translating Women* (University of Ottawa Press 2011).

Lia Hills is a poet, novelist and translator. Her work, including a libretto for a modern ballet, *Les Portes du Monde*, performed in Switzerland in 2007, has been published, performed and translated around the world. Recent publications include her prize-winning poetry collection, *the possibility of flight* (2008) and her novel, *The Beginner's Guide to Living* (2009), which was shortlisted for the Victorian, Queensland and Western Australian Premier's Literary Awards, among others. Her French–English translation of Marie Darrieussecq's acclaimed novel, *Tom is Dead*, has been described as 'a text as powerful as the original'. Lia is editor and co-initiator of *Moving Galleries*, a poetry-art project on Melbourne's trains.

Author **Elizabeth Honey** grew up on a farm near Wonthaggi and went on to study art, majoring in film and television, at Swinburne University in Melbourne. A writer, illustrator and poet, she has 17 titles to her name including *45 + 47 Stella Street and everything that happened*, *Honey Sandwich* and *Don't Pat the Wombat!*, all of which were Honour Books in the Children's Book Council of Australia Awards, and *Not a Nibble!*, winner of the CBCA Picture Book Award. Elizabeth's novels are recognised internationally: *45 + 47 Stella Street* won the Premio Cento Prize for Children's Literature (Italy), *Remote Man* was short listed for the Kinderliteraturpreis (Germany), and *To the Boy in Berlin*, written with Heike Brandt, was selected for The White Ravens, International Youth Library, Munich. Her most recent books, *That's not a Daffodil!* and *Ten Blue Wrens*, are both picture books.

Ouyang Yu came to Australia at the age of 35 and, now 56, has published 59 books of poetry, fiction, non-fiction, literary translation and criticism in English and Chinese, including the following: his award-winning novel, *The Eastern Slope Chronicle* (2002); his collection of poetry in English, *The Kingsbury Tales* (2008); his collection of Chinese poetry, *Slow Motion* (2009); his book of creative non-fiction, *On the Smell of an Oily Rag: Speaking English, Thinking Chinese and Living Australian* (2008); his second novel, *The English Class* (2010), which won the Community Relations Commission

Award in the 2011 New South Wales Premier's Literary Awards, as well as being short-listed for the 2011 Western Australia and Queensland Premier's Awards; his book of literary criticism, *Chinese in Australian Fiction: 1888–1988* (2008); and his translation in Chinese, *The Fatal Shore* (forthcoming in 2012). Ouyang Yu was nominated as one of the Top 100 Melburnians for 2011.

Rita Wilson is Associate Professor and currently Head of the School of Languages, Cultures and Linguistics at Monash University (Melbourne). Her research interests are both interdisciplinary and intercultural, combining literary and translation theories with studies of contemporary Italian literature and culture (with a particular focus on women writers), and investigating questions of transnational identity. Recent publications include *Words, Images and Performances in Translation*, co-edited with Brigid Maher (London and New York: Continuum, 2011), and several articles on the relationship between writing, (self-)translation and autobiography.